LEGACIES

Kermit Frazier

I0139518

BROADWAY PLAY PUBLISHING INC
New York
www.broadwayplaypublishing.com
info@broadwayplaypublishing.com

First printing: May 2013
I S B N: 978-0-88145-569-4

Book design: Marie Donovan
Page make-up: Adobe Indesign
Typeface: Palatino

ABOUT THE AUTHOR

Kermit Frazier's plays have been produced in New York and around the country at such theaters as the Milwaukee Repertory Theater, Asolo Repertory Theatre, Seattle Children's Theatre, First Stage Children's Theater, Baltimore Centerstage, the Philadelphia Drama Guild, the Ensemble Studio Theatre, and the New Federal Theatre. His plays include KERNEL OF SANITY, DINAH WASHINGTON IS DEAD, CLASS REUNION, SHADOWS AND ECHOES, INTERSTICES, LEGACIES, AN AMERICAN JOURNEY, DREAM KING, SACRED PLACES, LITTLE ROCK, and SMOLDERING FIRES. He has also written for such series as *Gullah Gullah Island* (Co-producer and Executive Story Editor), *The Cosby Mysteries, The Magic School Bus, The Misadventures of Maya and Miguel, The Wonder Pets,* and *All My Children.* He was a creator of and head writer for the popular children's mystery series, *Ghostwriter.* "Drive," the first chapter of his memoir, was published in *Callaloo.* Other articles, reviews, and short stories have appeared in such magazines and journals as *Green Mountains Review, The Chicago Review, American Theater, Black World, Essence,* and *The New York Times Book Review.* He has had fellowships at the Blue Mountain Center, MacDowell Colony, Yaddo, Millay Colony, Norton Island Residency, and the Liguria Study Center for the Arts and Humanities in Bogliasco, Italy. He teaches in the M F A Program in Creative Writing at Adelphi University.

LEGACIES was first produced at the Asolo Repertory Theatre (Artistic Director, Margaret Booker; Producer, Esther M Mertz) in Sarasota, Florida, in spring 1993. The cast and creative contributions were:

FRANKLIN THOMPSON III............................ George Merritt
DIANE THOMPSON.................................. Kim Brockington
BOBBY THOMPSON .... David Rainey
WANDA GENTRY...Leah Maddrie
JOSEPH GENTRY.. French Napier
CARLENE WALLACE ....Fanni Green
CARLETON WALLACE........................ John Canada Terrell
ROLAND BATTLES .... Charles Weldon
YOUNG FRANKLIN .... David Rainey
YOUNG CARLENE...Leah Maddrie
FRANKLIN THOMPSON, JR ....Clark Morgan

Director...Margaret Booker
Scenic design..G W Mercier
Lighting design ....Robert Wierzel
Costume Design...Judy Dearing
Composer/Arranger ....Baikida Carroll
Production Stage Manager ....Marian Wallace
Production Supervisor................................. Victor Meyrich
Assistant to the Stage Manager...................... Heather May

CHARACTERS & SETTING

FRANKLIN THOMPSON, III, *African American male, 53 years old*
DIANE THOMPSON, *African American female, 46 years old*
BOBBY THOMPSON, *African American male, 23 years old*
WANDA GENTRY, *African American female, 35 years old*
JOSEPH GENTRY, *African American male, 16 years old*
CARLENE WALLACE, *African American female, 53 years old*
CARLETON WALLACE, *African American male, 27 years old*
ROLAND BATTLES, *African American male, 47 years old*
FRANKIE, FRANKLIN *at 17 years old [played by actor who plays* BOBBY]
CARLIE, CARLENE *at 17 years old [played by actress who plays* WANDA]
FRANKLIN THOMPSON, JR., *African American male, 70's [voice only]*

The Time: Fall, 1983

The Place: FRANKLIN's *study and various other places both indoors and out in Northeastern U S A*

For my parents
Martha Davis and Bernard Ford Frazier

ACT ONE

(The stage has several levels that provide several playing areas. Center stage is FRANKLIN's *study, in which there are a large desk, a comfortable office chair that swivels, and books and papers spread and piled all around. That special space remains fixed throughout the play. All other places are represented by a minimum of furniture and props.)*

(As the music rises, the lights come up slowly to reveal FRANKLIN THOMPSON, III, *a 53-year-old African American man, asleep at his desk, papers and books spread over it.)*

(Soon the music segues into the booming voice of an African American Baptist preacher. He is FRANKLIN's *father.)*

FRANKLIN THOMPSON, JR: *(V O)* And so I just wanna remind you, son. You've gotta keep following that righteous path. That glorious, righteous path that's laid out so long and straight and narrow before you. 'Cause it's clear, it's good, and it goes way on back. Just turn your head if you don't believe me. Turn your head and see your granddaddy. And then look straight on at me. And then right on inside yourself. 'Cause it's gotta be right in there now, right on at you now… You can't shirk it, can't up and will it away. It runs through you like rich, strong blood. Anything else'll just lay you down low. Bring you up short. Put your life on empty. Keep you thrashing all 'round and 'round in the wilderness. Just mark my words, son! Mark every single one of these God-given, wonderful words!

FRANKLIN: *(Jerking awake)* What?!

(FRANKLIN takes a moment to come down from the dream. Meanwhile, DIANE, his wife, a 46- year-old African American woman, comes to the door of the study. She's dressed in a business suit. He looks at the books and papers on his desk, picking up a couple of them.)

FRANKLIN: Words.

DIANE: *(Calling)* Franklin?

FRANKLIN: Yes?

(DIANE enters the study.)

DIANE: Are you okay?

FRANKLIN: Yeah, I'm all right.

DIANE: You didn't come to bed last night.

FRANKLIN: I was working.

DIANE: Yeah, well…

(FRANKLIN returns to his work.)

DIANE: Are you eating breakfast today?

FRANKLIN: I'll grab something later.

DIANE: You ought to eat.

FRANKLIN: I will.

DIANE: When?

FRANKLIN: Diane, I don't— *(Returning to his work)* Before I go, okay?

DIANE: Did it ever occur to you that maybe, just maybe, you've bitten off a little more than you can chew this time?

FRANKLIN: What do you mean?

DIANE: The commute to City.

FRANKLIN: It's only a hundred miles or so, for God's sake.

DIANE: A two-hour drive.

FRANKLIN: Hour and a half.

DIANE: Two round-trips a week.

FRANKLIN: What do you want me to do? Stay over Tuesday through Thursday? I thought you didn't want that.

DIANE: I didn't. But if it would make you less tired all the time—

FRANKLIN: I'm not tired all the time.

DIANE: Come on, honey. You're going to have an accident one of these evenings coming back home. You're just three weeks into the semester and already—

FRANKLIN: *(Getting up from his desk)* All right, all right. So where would I stay that wouldn't cost an arm and a leg? And don't say with Battles.

DIANE: Why not with Battles?

FRANKLIN: Because we'd drive each other crazy. Anyway, I'd probably cramp his style.

DIANE: *(Knowingly)* Uh-huh.

FRANKLIN: Besides, my work is here.

DIANE: *(Looking around the study)* Yes…here.

FRANKLIN: I need to have ready access, you know that. This book's not gonna write itself.

DIANE: I know.

(DIANE kisses FRANKLIN and then he sits back down at his desk to continue working.)

DIANE: I've got to get to the office early. More change-ups in the Willis lawsuit. *(Heading for the door)* Oh and don't forget that Luella comes today. If you don't want her to "straighten up" in here, lock the door.

FRANKLIN: Why can't she just remember?

DIANE: Because she's compulsive. Which is the best kind of housekeeper to have. Will you be home for dinner?

FRANKLIN: Will you be home to cook it?

(DIANE *turns back to* FRANKLIN.)

FRANKLIN: Law practice, town council meetings.

DIANE: Point taken. But *I'm* still available.

(DIANE *exits. Franklin turns to see that she's gone and then turns back to his work. He picks up a page of text.*)

FRANKLIN: *(Reading)* "William Faulkner and Contemporary Afro-American Novelists: The Ineluctable Stream of Imagination and Memory." *(He crumples up the page in exasperation.)*

(*Lights fade out on* FRANKLIN's *study and come up on* WANDA's *living room, which is suggested by a couch, a coffee table, and an end table on which sits a double frame of photographs of young black men—one in an Army and one in a Marine uniform.* WANDA, *an African American woman just shy of 35 years old, is there, dressed for work.*)

WANDA: *(Calling)* Joseph, I don't wanna have to call you again, you hear? …Joseph!

(JOSEPH *comes in dressed in his pajamas. He is a 16 year-old African American boy.*)

WANDA: You're gonna look mighty foolish walking outta here like that.

JOSEPH: I don't feel good.

WANDA: What's that supposed to mean?

JOSEPH: My head aches.

WANDA: What, you hit your head on the bedpost or something?

JOSEPH: I'm serious, Mama. I'm sick.

WANDA: You seemed to bounce on in here all right last night.

JOSEPH: I tell you—

WANDA: Let me see. *(Feeling his forehead)* You don't have a fever.

JOSEPH: Why is it you gotta have a fever to be sick?

WANDA: You're going to school.

JOSEPH: But—

WANDA: You're going to school and that's that. Now go get some clothes on before you make me late.

JOSEPH: I ain't stoppin' you from going to work.

WANDA: Look, I wanna see your behind dressed and in front of me when I head out that door.

JOSEPH: Mama, I tell you I got a splittin' headache.

WANDA: Then take some aspirin. It wouldn't ache so much if you got up in time to eat your breakfast.

JOSEPH: I don't need me no breakfast. All I need is some more rest. *(He doesn't move.)*

WANDA: Why you still standing there?

JOSEPH: 'Cause I hate school, that's why. I hate it. *You* know I hate it. *I* know I hate it. My *teachers* know I hate it. Practically the whole *world* knows I hate it. And yet here I am back in it again. And that's how come I got me a headache.

(WANDA just looks at JOSEPH for a moment.)

WANDA: How old are you?

JOSEPH: *(Sighing deeply)* Mama, you know how—

WANDA: How *old*?

JOSEPH: Sixteen.

WANDA: Barely. And what grade are you in now?

JOSEPH: Tenth.

WANDA: And why are you in the tenth grade for the second time?

JOSEPH: This is ridiculous. You know why—

WANDA: Say it.

JOSEPH: *(Taking his time)* 'Cause I flunked last year.

WANDA: And what do you think would happen to you if you just walked away from school now?

JOSEPH: Nothin'.

WANDA: Oh, really? And how would you live on the "nothin"?

JOSEPH: I'd get me a job.

WANDA: Doing what?

JOSEPH: I—

WANDA: That's legal.

JOSEPH: I don't know. Any ole—

WANDA: Case closed. Get your clothes on.

JOSEPH: You don't understand, you know that? You just don't understand.

WANDA: Oh, I understand, all right. I understand plenty. It's Corey and M G and Short Stuff and whoever else you hang out with that ain't in school. Hangin' out with them when you outta be home doin' your school work like I say.

JOSEPH: Aw, Mama, that stuff's wack.

WANDA: No, I'll tell you what's "wack". Smoking reefer down on Eckert Avenue. That's what's wack.

JOSEPH: I wasn't—

WANDA: Don't lie to me, Joseph. And that, as a matter of fact, is probably where all your headaches come from.

JOSEPH: *(Under his breath)* Shit.

WANDA: What?

JOSEPH: Nothin'.

WANDA: It damn well better be nothin' or I'll— *(She takes a moment.)* Listen, I know how hard it is for you at times. But you've got to stick with it. And when you need some help just ask for it. I told you I'd help you out whenever I could, didn't I?

(JOSEPH sucks on his teeth in disapproval.)

WANDA: And if you don't want your mama looking over your shoulder then call the McKinney boy. He did offer to tutor you, you know.

(JOSEPH says nothing.)

WANDA: Well?

JOSEPH: I don't know.

WANDA: Joseph, don't do this to yourself.

JOSEPH: I ain't doin' nothin' to myself.

WANDA: Then who is? Who? Me? The school?

JOSEPH: They don't know how to teach nothin' at that school.

WANDA: *(With a sigh)* Get your clothes on, son. Please. *(Going to him)* We'll talk about this some more tonight after my class… Come on. You and me.

(Laughter is heard in another area of the stage as JOSEPH reluctantly exits with Wanda and lights cross fade to FRANKLIN and ROLAND BATTLES, a 49-year-old African American man. They are sitting in Battles' den, which is suggested by two lounge chairs. Each of them has a drink in his hand.)

FRANKLIN: Really?

BATTLES: I kid you not, man. And on top of that I hear that when he teaches his Milton class he's got a stick so far up his ass you can actually see the tip of it in his mouth when he opens it to speak.

(BATTLES *and* FRANKLIN *laugh.*)

BATTLES: Stewart's a real trip... Still, it ain't like the old days.

FRANKLIN: Nope.

BATTLES: Most of us scrunched up together on those H B C U campuses. About two and a half inches, max, from each other's dirty linen. Woo, what a stink... Now we've got to go to conferences and symposiums and shit to get the latest dope.

FRANKLIN: Or swing visiting professorships at each other's "white" universities.

BATTLES: Yeah, well, I tried to get the chumps to just flat out offer you a permanent position here, but Bateman's only half dead. Unfortunately, he'll rise from the ashes of his sabbatical next year. Besides, I think they'd be scared shitless to have two full-professor niggers permanently in the same department. Might spell revolution.

FRANKLIN: Humph.

BATTLES: Barrel-chested, atavistic, white male intellectuals complete with grunts and groans.

FRANKLIN: It's called preserving Western civilization.

BATTLES: It's called preserving your damn power base, that's what it's called. Which is tantamount to preserving your proverbial ass. But then you should know more about it than me, good buddy.

FRANKLIN: Why's that?

BATTLES: Being actually ensconced at private, pristine little Cannon College like you are.

FRANKLIN: It's not pristine.

BATTLES: *(Pressing on)* After all, City College here is just a good ole urban public institution with more minority students and part-time students and evening students and "older" students than it knows what to do with. Half the faculty complaining all the time about having to teach remedial this and remedial that just to accommodate "them".

FRANKLIN: Us.

BATTLES: *You* folks.

(BATTLES *and* FRANKLIN *laugh. Then* FRANKLIN *gets up and moves slightly away.* BATTLES *raises his glass.)*

BATTLES: Here's to the university life. All peaches and cream. Or is that Peaches and Herb?

FRANKLIN: Do you know why I really took this job?

BATTLES: Yeah. To hang out with me.

FRANKLIN: No, seriously.

BATTLES: That's not serious?

(FRANKLIN *gives* BATTLES *a look.)*

BATTLES: All right. Why?

FRANKLIN: I was feeling stuck. Thought maybe a temporary change of venue would help. But so far it hasn't.

BATTLES: Hey, man, cut yourself some slack, will you?

FRANKLIN: Words, Battles, words. I can't seem to find them anymore. They don't come together, don't shape themselves into anything that makes sense to me. What if the words start failing me completely? Then I'll have nothing, I'll disappear, I'll—

BATTLES: Hey, hey, ease up behind that. I haven't written a decent thing in years and I'm still here.

FRANKLIN: *(Kidding)* That's 'cause you're a slacking-off, no-count, knucklehead of a scholar.

BATTLES: *(Laughing)* Drop the "scholar" part and you'll have it down.

(FRANKLIN laughs half-heartedly, then grows somber again.)

BATTLES: Hey, the words'll flow again. And if they don't...well, there's always your family. Your wife, your son. They sure as hell aren't gonna let you disappear, believe me. Shit, divorce don't even cut them strings.

FRANKLIN: My family...Diane is out there wrapped up in one case after another all the time. And Bobby, well, you know how far out there *he* is.

BATTLES: Hey, props to Diane. As for Bobby...you could go "out there" and see him.

FRANKLIN: No.

BATTLES: Why not?

FRANKLIN: I don't have the time.

BATTLES: Make the time.

FRANKLIN: No. He won't come here, so why should I go there?

BATTLES: Because you're his father.

FRANKLIN: And how often do you see your kids?

BATTLES: I see them often enough.

FRANKLIN: Besides, who was it who flunked out of college after just one semester? Who was it who spent most of his time doped up on all kinds of mess?

BATTLES: Yeah, but—

FRANKLIN: And then coming in my study like that. Ripping up my books, my papers. My soul. Like he was trying to rip out my soul. So let him stay out there, screw up his life, ruin his reputation.

(Slight pause)

BATTLES: He's your flesh and blood, man.

(Slight pause)

FRANKLIN: Flesh and blood. Just like my father. Franklin Thompson, Jr. An eight-five-year-old junior… The last time I went to see him he said nothing to me. Absolutely nothing. Just stared and stared. *(Slight pause)* I don't know. It's like I'm suddenly glimpsing the end of this road. A road I thought was much longer, much wider. And something inside of me is whispering: "Turn. You missed a turn."

(Suddenly, voices are heard U R in the dark.)

CARLETON: Fifty dollars, Mama. Just fifty measly ole dollars.

CARLENE: I don't have fifty dollars to be giving away to you.

(Lights come up U R on a living room as they fade out on BATTLES' den. The living room is suggested by a couch and chair. CARLENE, a 53-year-old African American woman, is there with her son CARLETON, a 27-years-old African American.)

CARLETON: A loan. Not a gift.

CARLENE: A loan? Shoot, you don't know what the word "loan" means.

CARLETON: Aw, Mama, I'll pay you back. I swear.

CARLENE: Ain't no use in swearin' it 'cause both you and me know it ain't gonna happen.

CARLETON: Well, I try, don't I? Don't I always be tryin'?

CARLENE: You don't try hard enough for either one of us.

CARLETON: Yes, I do. 'Sides, what's fifty dollars when it comes to your only survivin' son? Don't I deserve a little somethin' from you every now and again?

CARLENE: Now I hope you not sayin' that I haven't given you even *more* than a little somethin' over the past twenty-seven years of your existence on this earth. I hope you not sayin' that. Not to my face.

CARLETON: No, I'm not sayin' that.

CARLENE: Then what *are* you sayin'?

CARLETON: *(Hesitating)* I…I need me fifty dollars. Plain and simple.

CARLENE: For what?

CARLETON: Why I gotta be tellin' you for what for?

CARLENE: 'Cause all money usually do is turn to liquor five minutes after it done dropped into your hands.

CARLETON: I'm not talkin' about no liquor. 'Sides, you drink. Daddy drank.

CARLENE: Your daddy's dead from it, too.

CARLETON: You're not.

CARLENE: I'm not no alcoholic.

CARLETON: Neither am I.

CARLENE: You a fool for denying it. Just like your daddy was.

CARLETON: Mama, let's not get into this, okay? I'm talkin' about a loan to help me pay a debt I owe, okay? That's what I'm talkin' about.

CARLENE: What kind of debt?

CARLETON: A small bet I made, that's all. Just a small little side bet.

CARLENE: Carleton, you too old for this foolishness.

CARLETON: What's age got to do with it? 'Sides, you play the numbers.

CARLENE: Not fifty dollars and up at a shot. If you spent as much time and energy holdin' on to a job as you do schemin' and dealin' you wouldn't have these kinds of debt problems.

CARLETON: Aw, Mama, ain't no big deal. Everybody's in debt. Even the rich boys in they own way. Profit/loss, deficit spendin'. So that ain't the real deal. It's how your work through it, make use of it. How you flip and roll your figures.

CARLENE: Yeah, well, it don't seem like you been flippin' and rollin' too good lately.

CARLETON: Just a minor snag, that's all. Just a little bitty ole snag.

CARLENE: Uh-huh. So what's the matter with your job at the cleaners?

CARLETON: You want a list?

CARLENE: Don't you quit that job.

CARLETON: I ain't say nothin' about quittin'. But you got to know I'm not gonna be workin' in no hot, steamy cleaners for the rest of my life neither.

CARLENE: Right now I'd just settle for six months.

CARLETON: Probably won't even be that long.

CARLENE: Why? Where you goin'?

CARLETON: Where you *think* I'm goin'?

CARLENE: Owin' me fifty dollars?

CARLETON: You ain't loan it to me yet.

CARLENE: And I'm not gonna loan it to you neither. Now you just keep your job, collect your paycheck,

stay out the liquor store, pay your rent, and pay your
debts. And just forget about this goin' to California.
Don't see why you wanna be goin' all the way out
there anyway. Ain't nothin' so special out there as far
as I can see. Exceptin' maybe earthquakes. And then
that'd be that. 'Sides, you been "goin' to California"
for the past two years. Ain't even made it half out the
neighborhood yet.

CARLETON: Why you doubtin' me? Why you all the
time gotta be—

(The door buzzer sounds four times in a special rhythm.)

CARLENE: That's Wanda. If you was smart you'd stop
all this tap dancin' and go back to school like your
sister.

CARLETON: Humph… How come you won't never give
me the key to here?

CARLENE: 'Cause ain't no need in you bein' here when
I'm not. What you gonna do? Cook and clean for me
while I'm out doin' it for other folks?

CARLETON: I might would if you give me fifty dollars.

CARLENE: Oh, so now it's "give" me.

CARLETON: You know what I—

(WANDA enters.)

CARLETON: Well, looka here, looka here. Miss College
Girl Wanda back from big-time City College.

WANDA: You know I could hear your voice clear down
the hall.

CARLETON: But you couldn't hear Mama's, is that it?

WANDA: *(Ignoring CARLETON)* Hi, Mama.

CARLENE: Hi, baby.

CARLETON: Well, that's all right. 'Cause that's the way
it's supposed to be anyway, girl. I mean I *am* the man

in this family, you know. The *man*. So my voice is
supposed to be carryin' further.

WANDA: What's the matter, Mama?

CARLETON: Ain't nothin' the matter, Sis. Me and Mama
was just conversatin', that's all. Just havin' ourselves a
little tête-a-tête.

CARLENE: I think you'd better go home now, Carleton.

CARLETON: Mama, I need me fifty—

CARLENE: Did you hear what I said?

(CARLETON *looks back and forth between* CARLENE *and*
WANDA *for a moment.*)

CARLETON: I don't get it sometimes. I really don't. I
ain't all that no count, you know. It ain't like I'm rottin'
on the damn vine or somethin'. But can I help it if I
been stabbed in the heart?

(CARLENE *and* WANDA *have heard all this before.*)

CARLETON: Can I help that? ...But hey, that's all right.
That's all right. 'Cause me, I'm gettin' out soon. Gettin'
clean on outta here. Gonna find me a place where I can
breathe, where I can be myself. (*He exits.*)

CARLENE: Maybe I should have just given him the
money.

WANDA: No. You promised yourself, remember? No
more proppin' him up.

CARLENE: But he's my baby.

WANDA: Mama, he's a grown man. A grown man with
a self-inflicted wound he won't—

CARLENE: It's not all that self-inflicted, Wanda. Now
you know that.

WANDA: Maybe not. But he won't let it heal. Just keeps
pickin' at it and pullin' the stitches out and rubbin' dirt
all up in it. Ain't nobody's fault but his own now.

CARLENE: Yeah, I guess you're right. Miss College Girl.

WANDA: *(Uncertain)* College girl, all right.

CARLENE: What's the matter?

WANDA: I don't know if I'm gonna be able to make it through this college stuff.

CARLENE: 'Course you are.

WANDA: I'm already behind. And I'm just takin' two courses. Shoot, I know a couple of people who're takin' four.

CARLENE: Workin' full time?

WANDA: Yes.

CARLENE: With a teenage son at home?

WANDA: At home? Don't I wish.

CARLENE: What do you mean?

WANDA: When I got home this evening he wasn't even there. Made me so mad.

CARLENE: He's probably out with his friends.

WANDA: I specifically told him to stay home and study.

CARLENE: Maybe he'd already finished.

WANDA: Yeah, and I'm Tina Turner. This is crazy, you know that? Crazy. *I'm* out so *he's* out. Here I am going back to school and I can't even... I got a "D+" on my last English assignment. Got a "D" on the first one.

CARLENE: Well...you improvin'.

WANDA: How am I gonna be settin' a good example for Joseph if I'm bringin' home nothin' but—

CARLENE: But you not in college for Joseph. You in college for yourself.

WANDA: Still, if I quit so soon, how can I be tellin' him to—

CARLENE: First off, you not gonna quit. You just tired, that's all. Just a little tired. I mean it's all new. *New.* And what if you did eventually quit? What's that got to do with Joseph? He's a child. A black child who oughtta at least graduate from high school. Just like you and Eddie done.

(WANDA *smiles.*)

WANDA: Eddie…I miss him, too, you know. Just as much as Carleton does sometimes.

CARLENE: So do I, baby, so do I.

WANDA: I'm scared, Mama. Scared for my son. I don't wanna lose him.

(*Lights fade out on* CARLENE's *living room as a spotlight comes up D S on* FRANKLIN. *He is standing before his contemporary Afro-American literature class.*)

FRANKLIN: Hence, in John Wideman's fiction, as in some of the other Afro-American writers we'll explore this semester, we glimpse two major concerns: the significance of history in our lives and the ever-presence of a working imagination. In fact, these concerns are entangled in a kind of symbiotic relationship. The imagination tries to sort out and come to grips with history, with the past, in order to make viable the present, make possible the future. History, in turn—

(*Suddenly,* FRANKLIN's *father's voice begins to insinuate itself.*)

FRANKLIN THOMPSON JR: (*V O*) Preach, son, preach.

(FRANKLIN *tries to press on, but his father's voice continues to interfere with and overlap his own, causing him to be increasingly agitated and disoriented.*)

FRANKLIN: Uh…history, in turn…

FRANKLIN THOMPSON JR: *(V O)* Give the church and family what they need.

FRANKLIN: ...influences how the imagination...

FRANKLIN THOMPSON JR: *(V O)* Continuity, strength.

FRANKLIN: ...perceives the present...

FRANKLIN THOMPSON JR: *(V O)* You can't shirk it...

FRANKLIN: ...and how it projects...

FRANKLIN THOMPSON JR: *(V O)* ...can't up and will it away...

FRANKLIN: ...itself into the future...

FRANKLIN THOMPSON JR: *(V O)* ...runs through you like rich, strong blood.

FRANKLIN: *(Bursting out)* Stop this!

(FRANKLIN's father's voice falls silent. Now FRANKLIN is aware again that he's lecturing.)

FRANKLIN: *(Embarrassed)* I'm so sorry... Class is nearly over. Let's just continue next time. *(He practically flees the classroom.)*

(WANDA enters. She's in a corridor of a floor on which much of the English Department at City College is housed. She's looking for a particular office.)

(FRANKLIN enters in a rush and passes WANDA without noticing her.)

WANDA: *(Turning)* Excuse me.

(FRANKLIN keeps going.)

WANDA: Excuse me, sir. Uh, professor.

(FRANKLIN stops and turns back to WANDA.)

FRANKLIN: Yes?

(FRANKLIN is suddenly taken aback by WANDA, this young woman he doesn't know. Something about her, something

in her face, strikes a deep cord within him, but he doesn't know why. He remains riveted through the next few lines of dialogue.)

WANDA: Would you happen to know where Professor Rifkin's office is?

FRANKLIN: Who?

WANDA: Professor Rifkin. He teaches English one-ten.

FRANKLIN: One-ten?

WANDA: Yes. Tuesdays at six.

(FRANKLIN *just keeps staring.)*

WANDA: Professor?

FRANKLIN: *(Coming out of it)* Oh, I'm sorry.

WANDA: Is something wrong?

FRANKLIN: Uh…no. I just…saw something. In my head. I'm sorry. What did you ask me?

WANDA: Where I could find Professor Rifkin's office.

FRANKLIN: Rifkin?

WANDA: Yes. A young white man. Dark hair. Glasses. He's a part-time teacher here, I think.

FRANKLIN: Oh, an adjunct, you mean.

WANDA: I guess.

FRANKLIN: No, I don't know him.

WANDA: Oh.

FRANKLIN: Why don't you check in the English department office?

WANDA: *(Somewhat embarrassed)* I couldn't find it.

FRANKLIN: You go through the doors at the end of the hall and then up the stairs to the next floor.

WANDA: Oh, no wonder. I'm on the wrong floor. I'm sorry.

FRANKLIN: That's all right.

WANDA: Thank you.

FRANKLIN: Sure.

(WANDA *turns to go.*)

FRANKLIN: Miss.

WANDA: *(Turning back)* Yes?

FRANKLIN: Have we...have we met before?

WANDA: No, I don't think so.

FRANKLIN: At another college maybe.

WANDA: No.

FRANKLIN: Are you sure?

WANDA: This is my first semester in any college.

FRANKLIN: Oh.

(FRANKLIN *and* WANDA *just look at each other for an awkward moment.*)

WANDA: Wanda Gentry.

FRANKLIN: I beg your pardon.

WANDA: I'm Wanda Gentry, Professor...

FRANKLIN: Oh, Thompson. Franklin Thompson. Look, I'm sorry about all this staring.

WANDA: That's all right. In fact, it's even nice sometimes.

(WANDA *exits S L, as* FRANKLIN *stares after her.*)

FRANKLIN: Wanda Gentry.

(FRANKLIN *exits S R as lights come up on* DIANE, *who is at home talking on the telephone.*)

DIANE: No, no, I don't think we should deal that way. I mean, if he's going to take that kind of attitude then we should get somebody else for the job... Uh-huh... Yes, of course.

(FRANKLIN *enters. He and* DIANE *acknowledge each other. Then* FRANKLIN *goes straight to his study.*)

DIANE: Yes, Myron, just like I said... Well, I'm the committee chairperson. It's up to me to decide that. Yes! ...Yes, Myron, yes...

(*As* DIANE *listens impatiently on the phone,* FRANKLIN *sits deep in thought.*)

DIANE: Look it's sort of late. Why don't you call me at the office in the morning? Maybe we can straighten this out then... Great. Bye.

(DIANE *hangs up the phone and then hurries to* FRANKLIN'*s study.*)

FRANKLIN: (*To himself*) Carlene?!

DIANE: (*Outside the door of the study*) Franklin?

(FRANKLIN *is at first disoriented, as though* CARLENE *has responded to his calling out her name.*)

FRANKLIN: (*In a desperate whisper*) Carly...

DIANE: (*Calling*) Franklin.

FRANKLIN: (*Reorienting himself*) Yes, come in, Diane.

DIANE: (*Entering excitedly*) Guess what?

FRANKLIN: (*Distracted*) What?

DIANE: We won a decision in the Willis case!

FRANKLIN: Are you serious?

DIANE: Yes! The judge suddenly threw out the lawsuit.

FRANKLIN: (*Hugging her*) That's so great.

DIANE: Isn't it? All that pushing I did. All the motions and depositions and filings. All worth it. My approach. *Mine.*

FRANKLIN: You're one bright woman.

DIANE: Thank you, thank you, thank you.

(FRANKLIN *suddenly returns to thoughts of* CARLENE *and* WANDA.)

DIANE: What's the matter, honey? Rough day?

FRANKLIN: No, I'm okay. Just work.

DIANE: *(Kissing him)* You and me. Doing what we do. Just wish Bobby was back home. That would complete the picture.

FRANKLIN: *(Unconvinced)* Yeah.

DIANE: Come on, Franklin. He's our only child. Sometimes I wish we would've, could've had more. But he's all we've got.

FRANKLIN: Yeah.

DIANE: Well, he'll come back when he's ready. Meanwhile, mister, we've got to celebrate! Tonight!

FRANKLIN: *(Not wanting to)* Oh, honey—

DIANE: Come on.

FRANKLIN: It's kinda late. And I've got to get through this one section of the manuscript.

DIANE: One night. *(Seductively)* Come on, treats all around. *(Kissing him on each word)* Before, during *and* after.

FRANKLIN: *(Drawn in)* Well…when you put it that way.

DIANE: *(Beckoning)* I'll go change.

FRANKLIN: I'll…I'll help you.

(DIANE *smiles and heads out, but instead of following her,* FRANKLIN *stares D S.)*

FRANKLIN: Wanda Gentry.

(FRANKLIN *leaves his study but exits in the opposite direction of* DIANE. *Then rap music suddenly blasts as the lights fade out on* FRANKLIN'*s study and come up on* WANDA'*s living room, where* JOSEPH *is jamming to the music from a boom box he's brought in, rapping along. Soon* FRANKLIN *and* WANDA *enter, but* JOSEPH *doesn't notice them.)*

WANDA: Joseph.

(JOSEPH *is oblivious.* WANDA *turns off the music on the boom box.)*

JOSEPH: Hey, what the hell's— *(Noticing he has company)* Oh.

WANDA: *(Half-seriously)* You know, somebody could break in here and rob us blind and you'd still be steady rappin' on.

JOSEPH: Sorry, Mama.

WANDA: This is Professor Thompson. He teaches in the English Department at City College. And he was nice enough to give me a ride home...Professor Thompson, my son Joseph.

FRANKLIN: *(Extending his hand)* Pleased to meet you, Joseph.

JOSEPH: *(Shaking* FRANKLIN'*s hand)* What's up...sir?

WANDA: You get your dinner?

JOSEPH: Yeah.

WANDA: Finish your homework?

JOSEPH: I was taking a break.

WANDA: Then maybe you'd better—

JOSEPH: Yeah, I know. *(He picks up his boom box and heads to his room.)*

WANDA: Let me know if you need any help.

FRANKLIN: Nice meeting you, Joseph.

(JOSEPH *is gone.*)

WANDA: Sixteen.

FRANKLIN: Yes.

WANDA: I try to keep on him about his school work, but it's sort of hard. He doesn't like "hanging around the house".

FRANKLIN: I know what you mean. I had a son like that.

WANDA: Had?

FRANKLIN: When he was living at home, I mean.

WANDA: I suppose it gets better when they "leave the nest".

FRANKLIN: *(With a laugh)* That's what they tell me.

WANDA: Like I said, I really do appreciate the ride. Oh, listen, would you like a snack or something to drink? I'm not sure what's here that Joseph hasn't already inhaled but—

FRANKLIN: No, thanks.

WANDA: Well, have a seat at least.

FRANKLIN: Just for a minute or so. Thanks.

(FRANKLIN *and* WANDA *sit on the sofa.*)

WANDA: Hope I didn't talk your head off in the car.

FRANKLIN: No.

WANDA: Me and this college thing.

FRANKLIN: I understand.

WANDA: Also nervousness, I guess.

FRANKLIN: How so?

WANDA: Never been in the same car with a college professor before. And a black one at that.

(FRANKLIN *simply smiles.*)

WANDA: I think it's really fascinating what you do. Not the teaching part, the writing. Not that teaching isn't fascinating but—

FRANKLIN: No, I understand.

WANDA: I've never met a writer. A creator of whole books.

FRANKLIN: "Whole books." ...When you put it that way I guess it is pretty fascinating, isn't it? But I don't really create that many whole books, believe me. I mostly write about them in tiny little fragments of thought and theory called articles. Or essays, if I'm feeling more self-important.

WANDA: It must be exciting to see your name in print.

FRANKLIN: As a matter of fact it *is* sort of exciting.

WANDA: Something lasting, permanent. Something to leave behind you when you go, to hand down to your kids maybe.

FRANKLIN: Yes.

(FRANKLIN *simply stares at* WANDA *for a moment, which makes her feel momentarily uncomfortable.*)

FRANKLIN: I'm serious about my offer, you know. Just stop by my office any Tuesday or Thursday.

WANDA: Well, I feel sort of honored, Professor, but are you sure—

FRANKLIN: Yes, it'd be my pleasure. And my way of looking at English composition again. Haven't taught it in so long. It'd be good for me.

WANDA: *And* me.

FRANKLIN: Yes, well, we all can use some help every once in a while, now can't we?

(Again FRANKLIN *simply stares at* WANDA, *which now causes her to smile. Now slightly embarrassed,* FRANKLIN *gets up, looking around as he does.)*

FRANKLIN: Nice place you've got here.

WANDA: No, it isn't. I need to move really. Need to be renting something a lot nicer. Something in a nicer neighborhood. Maybe even owning something… Dreams. Never had all that much really. You see, me and my son…well…

(To change the subject FRANKLIN *focuses on the double-framed photographs of the two young black men in uniform on the end table.)*

FRANKLIN: Those are nice pictures.

WANDA: Yes, they are, aren't they?

FRANKLIN: Your brothers?

WANDA: Only the one in the Marine uniform. *(Bringing the photos to* FRANKLIN*)* This one here. My half brother actually. Eddie. He was killed in Vietnam.

FRANKLIN: Oh, I'm sorry.

WANDA: Thank you. The other one's my father.

FRANKLIN: *(Taken aback)* Your father?

WANDA: Yes.

*(*FRANKLIN *stares at the photo.)*

WANDA: He died in Korea. I never knew him really. Just pieces of things. Snapshots. A couple of old letters. Stories from my mother. You see, I wasn't even two when he went overseas… His name was Joseph. My son's named after him.

FRANKLIN: I see.

*(*FRANKLIN *gives the photographs back to* WANDA.*)*

FRANKLIN: I'd better be heading home.

WANDA: Didn't mean to keep you.

FRANKLIN: You didn't. Until Thursday perhaps.

WANDA: Well...

FRANKLIN: That is, if you need some help.

WANDA: Oh, I'm sure I will.

FRANKLIN: Of course, I don't mean to be pushy.

WANDA: Oh, I know.

(FRANKLIN is nearly gone when he suddenly turns back to WANDA.)

FRANKLIN: Uh...listen. I hope you don't mind my asking, but would you satisfy a curiosity of mine and tell me what your mother's name is?

WANDA: My *mother's* name?

FRANKLIN: Yes.

WANDA: Carlene Wallace. Why? You think you might know her?

(WANDA waits for FRANKLIN to answer, but he is lost in the reality of his knowing that first name.)

WANDA: Professor?

FRANKLIN: *(Snapping out of it)* Oh, sorry. No, I don't know her. It's your eyes. They remind me of some of my mother's relatives.

WANDA: *(Laughing despite herself)* Oh, really? You mean we could be related way back when?

FRANKLIN: No, no, not at all. It was just a feeling I had, I guess.

WANDA: *(Only half-jokingly)* Well, I hope you're not too disappointed in me.

FRANKLIN: Oh, no, of course not.

WANDA: I mean you can still keep the feeling.

FRANKLIN: *(Hesitantly)* Yes. *(Shaking her hand)* Well, goodbye.

WANDA: Goodbye.

(FRANKLIN exits. Lights fade out on WANDA's living room as FRANKLIN reels into the street and heads home.)

(Simultaneously, the sound of a knife sticking into wood is heard. Lights come up on CARLETON and JOSEPH sitting on a park bench. CARLETON is flipping a shiny large pocket knife expertly into the bench. There is a pint of whiskey at CARLETON's feet.)

(It is evening.)

CARLETON: So ole Sis still steady on your case, huh?

JOSEPH: Yeah. *(He takes a joint out of his pocket and then searches for matches in another pocket.)*

CARLETON: Well, it bees dat way sometimes.

JOSEPH: *(Finding matches)* Yeah.

(JOSEPH lights the joint, takes a toke, and then offers it to CARLETON.)

CARLETON: Naw, naw, never touch the stuff. You know that. *(Picking up his pint of whiskey)* And neither should you, I might add. *(He takes a drink.)*

JOSEPH: Look who's talkin'.

CARLETON: Lookit, I'm a man, you still a boy, and liquor ain't dope. End of sermon.

(CARLETON and JOSEPH toke and drink.)

JOSEPH: I just want out, Uncle C, that's all. Out.

CARLETON: Yeah, well, I heard that.

JOSEPH: It's always Joseph this and Joseph that. Joseph, where you goin'? Joseph, where you been? Joseph, do this, that, or some other damn thing. Nothin' but Joseph, Joseph, Joseph.

(CARLETON *laughs.*)

CARLETON: Well, she can't help that none. Your name *is* Joseph.

JOSEPH: Yeah, well, maybe if I change my damn name she'd leave me the hell alone.

CARLETON: Now you know your mama wouldn't allow that 'cause she's got herself right where she wants to be. Between Joseph bookends. Past and future. Daddy and son.

JOSEPH: And what about *my* daddy?

CARLETON: Lionel? Shit, Lionel ain't hardly worried about you. Wherever he is.

JOSEPH: Yeah, well, I like "Lionel" better than "Joseph".

CARLETON: Why? 'Cause it sounds like "lion", or 'cause it reminds you of a little ole choo-choo train?

(Somewhat embarrassed, JOSEPH *just tokes on the joint.* CARLETON *laughs.)*

CARLETON: Names. Labels. Either we find them or they find us. *(He looks at the bench.)* Like for instance, take this shit carved here. What the hell is this anyway?… "Dookie loves Box." Now you tell me, who the hell's who in that relationship? *(With great fanfare)* What they hope or what they see. Or maybe what they long to be.

*(*CARLETON *hesitates and then flips the knife into the bench. He and* JOSEPH *stare at the knife until* JOSEPH *gets uncomfortable.)*

JOSEPH: Uh, Uncle C…

*(*CARLETON *quickly pulls the knife out of the bench and studies it.)*

CARLETON: "I'm gonna give you this, C." Eddie was the first one to call me "C."

JOSEPH: I know that, Uncle C.

CARLETON: "Give it to you for safekeeping, that is. So you just keep it for me, you here? For when I get back from Nam." ...He promised me he'd come back.

JOSEPH: I know, Uncle C.

CARLETON: Come back and reclaim his knife.

JOSEPH: I know.

CARLETON: It's been here ready and waitin'.

JOSEPH: Yeah.

CARLETON: Been here over ten years. February fifteenth, nineteen seventy-two. I was sixteen years old.

JOSEPH: *(Somewhat bored)* Yeah, you've told me that a few times already.

(CARLETON *quickly turns the knife on* JOSEPH, *who jumps back.)*

CARLETON: So what the hell are you all of a sudden? A fuckin' smartass?

JOSEPH: Naw!

CARLETON: Think you know all there is to know about it, is that it?

JOSEPH: Naw, naw, Uncle C. I don't think that.

(CARLETON *gets up and flips the knife into the bench right where he's been sitting.)*

CARLETON: Damn straight, you don't. 'Cause don't nobody know it all, you hear me? Nobody!

JOSEPH: Hey, I'm sorry.

CARLETON: Yeah, you sorry. We all sorry.

(CARLETON *turns D S away from* JOSEPH. JOSEPH *looks at the knife stuck in the bench as though he would like to pull it out and hide it, but he doesn't dare touch it.)*

CARLETON: I took me a bus trip to D C last weekend. Went there to see the Vietnam thing. The memorial.

Went by myself. Didn't tell nobody I was goin' 'cause I knew nobody woulda wanted to go with me anyway.

JOSEPH: I would've gone with you.

CARLETON: Yeah, well… It's been almost a year since it was dedicated so like it was about time, you know… But when I got to the Mall, well, I kinda got lost at first. Stumblin' all over the damn Monument grounds. Kept runnin' into all the wrong things. Fuckin' tourists and ducks and ponds and twisty paths and shit. But then finally: *boom*. There it was. Just over this one particular rise. And it was like a shock, you know. All gleaming in the sun. All stone-stiff and swept along the ground like the humongous wings of some damn dead airplane. Nose buried. Tail shot off and gone. And it really ain't all that crowded so I'm feelin' okay, you know. Kinda right, ready…I make my way to one of them books under glass at one of the entrances. Flip through the pages, find Eddie's name. And that sends me to the right panel and line, see. And hey, what do you know? I mean like what do you fuckin' know? Like he's just got to be in the middle, right? Almost stone dead in the middle of the whole goddam thing. *(He, still facing D S, is now "at the wall.")* And I…I get up close, see. Stand right before it. And I read…I read: Edward A Wallace, Junior. *(Lifting his right hand)* I lift my right hand and it starts shakin', shakin' like a damn leaf. And somethin' starts turnin' upside down in my guts. But I don't stop. *(Tracing the air)* 'Cause I've gotta do it. I've gotta trace every single letter in my big brother's name. 'Cause I'm hopin' that maybe it'd be over then, finished, all this crazy-assed shit inside of me. *(He stops tracing.)* But it don't work. It don't fuckin' work. *(He lets out a little laugh.)* And you wanna know why? 'Cause all the while I'm doin' it I can fuckin' see myself, man. *(He slowly begins backing U S away from "the wall".)* See myself right there in that glassy stone wall. My reflection lookin' back at me lookin' back at those goddam small-assed little chiseled letters.

(CARLETON turns to JOSEPH, who has not moved from his spot on the bench.)

CARLETON: Chiseled. *(He pulls the knife out of the bench.)* Chiseled. *(He raises the knife to his face and seems to be chiseling letters into his forehead as he speaks.)* Edward A Wallace, Jr. chiseled right across my own forehead. *(He lowers knife to his side.)* No escape, Little Joe. No fuckin' escape.

(Lights fade out on CARLETON and JOSEPH and come up on FRANKLIN and WANDA in her apartment. They sit on the sofa drinking coffee. A plate of cookies is on the coffee table along with a folder that has one of her papers in it.)

WANDA: So my mother, she's behind me all the way. *(Quoting her mother)* "You gonna be the first, girl. The first college graduate in our whole entire family! Ain't that gonna be somethin'!"

(WANDA laughs. FRANKLIN smiles.)

WANDA: Her eyes light up so much when she says that. She's worked so hard keeping the family together.

FRANKLIN: What does your mother do?

WANDA: She's a housekeeper. A domestic. Travels clear on out to the suburbs cleaning. Watching a coupla white kids grow up even as she watched us grow. But she's doing okay. *(Quoting again)* "Twice widowed and still gettin' up!" *(Smiling)* I like quoting her.

FRANKLIN: She sounds eminently quotable.

WANDA: *She* oughtta be the one in college.

FRANKLIN: Oh, come on now. I mean perhaps she should be, but so should you. You're a very bright young la— Woman. And as I said in my office, your paper really isn't that bad.

WANDA: Then how come it's got all these red marks all over it? Shoot, my instructor wrote more than I did.

FRANKLIN: He's just over-zealous, that's all. *(He takes her paper out of the folder.)* But your ideas are good. You just need to learn more about structure, shape, need some work on your grammar, need to be more careful about diction, be sure you're conveying exactly what you want to say.

WANDA: *(Sarcastically)* Oh, is that all?

FRANKLIN: No, no, you can do this, Wanda. Believe me, you *can*. I'm going to make sure you can because I'm— *(He catches himself.)* I'm a good teacher. Used to be anyway.

WANDA: I'm sure you still are.

FRANKLIN: So let's set up a schedule, why don't we? We can meet in my office, meet…here. Take this one step at a time. *(He holds out his hand.)*

WANDA: *(Shaking his hand)* All right.

(FRANKLIN exits.)

(There is a cacophonous swirl of music to indicate a passage of time. Then lights come up U R in the THOMPSON home. DIANE sits in a chair, looking over some legal documents and waiting for FRANKLIN to come home. It is late in the evening.)

(After a moment FRANKLIN comes in. He is surprised to see DIANE there.)

FRANKLIN: Hi.

(DIANE says nothing and doesn't look at FRANKLIN.)

FRANKLIN: Still working?

(Again DIANE says nothing. FRANKLIN goes to her and kisses her on the cheek. She accepts his kiss passively.)

FRANKLIN: It's kind of late. Aren't you tired? ...Well, I am. Battles and his last-minute get-togethers.

DIANE: Oops. You know, one of the first things you tell a client when you're prepping him to take the stand is to never volunteer information. Always wait for the question.

FRANKLIN: What?

DIANE: Where've you been?

FRANKLIN: Didn't your secretary give you my message?

DIANE: Yeah. So where've you been?

FRANKLIN: Over Battles. Just like I said.

DIANE: I called Battles.

FRANKLIN: And?

DIANE: He said you'd already left.

FRANKLIN: Then what's the—

DIANE: That was over three hours ago.

FRANKLIN: Well, you're the one always on my case about driving too fast.

(DIANE *is not amused.*)

FRANKLIN: All right, I stopped to get something to eat on the way home.

DIANE: I thought you ate at Battles.

FRANKLIN: Have you tried eating at Battles since he and Vickie got divorced?

DIANE: No, as a matter of fact, I haven't.

FRANKLIN: What's the problem?

DIANE: Who is she?

FRANKLIN: What are you talking about? Who's who?

DIANE: A student? Is she a student?

FRANKLIN: That's ridiculous.

DIANE: A month, Franklin. A month of late returns and increasingly lame excuses. A month of I'm working late and I'm speaking here and there and I've got this meeting and that meeting and Battles, hey, well, you know Battles, he's my buddy, my friend, my alibi and cover.

FRANKLIN: Look, I'm sorry I've been away so much lately but—

DIANE: No, uh-uh, that won't cut it.

FRANKLIN: Okay, then what about you? How often are *you* here? How many clients, how many court dates, how many council meetings are there anyway?

DIANE: That's not the—

FRANKLIN: Luella cleans the house, restaurants cook the food—

DIANE: And you're hardly in bed lately! *(Slight pause)* Do you love me?

FRANKLIN: Yes.

DIANE: Then tell me what's going on.

FRANKLIN: Nothing's going on.

(DIANE just looks at FRANKLIN, still not believing him. He doesn't back down. Finally, she gathers up her legal documents and exits.)

(FRANKLIN is caught in the dilemma of his lie.)

(There is a cacophonous swirl of music to indicate a passage of time as lights fade out on FRANKLIN's home and come up on CARLENE's apartment. CARLENE, CARLETON, JOSEPH, and WANDA are standing around a table on which sits a cake with three lighted candles as well as plates, cups, utelnsils, napkins, and a pitcher of Kool-aide. Meanwhile, FRANKLIN appears in a spotlight D S and observes the scene.)

CARLENE, CARLETON, *and* JOSPEH *cheer and applaud* WANDA.*)*

WANDA: Thank you so much!

WANDA: And let's skip that verse, okay? We all know how old I am.

CARLETON: Yeah, three candles' worth. One for each century.

*(*WANDA *bops* CARLETON *playfully.)*

JOSEPH: Blow out the candles, Mama, so we can eat.

CARLENE: Hold your water. She's gotta make a wish first.

*(*WANDA *closes her eyes and makes a wish. Then she opens them and blows out the candles.)*

JOSEPH: All right! Cut the cake.

WANDA: Where's the knife?

CARLENE: *(Starting for the kitchen)* Durn.

CARLETON: Wait, Mama, I got one. *(He takes his brother's knife out of his pocket.)* Eddie's.

CARLENE: Is it clean?

CARLETON: I keep it clean, Mama.

*(*CARLETON *opens it and holds it out to* WANDA, *who looks at* CARLENE, *who nods.* WANDA *takes the knife and begins cutting the cake. (To* WANDA*)* So what'd you wish for?

JOSEPH: She's not supposed to tell, Uncle C.

CARLETON: Probably for a way to finish college in less than twenty years.

CARLENE: Carleton.

CARLETON: Just kidding, Mama.

JOSEPH: Where's the ice cream?

CARLENE: Shoot, I'm forgetting everything this evening.

CARLETON: Hold it, Mama.

WANDA: Don't tell me you got *that* in your pocket, too.

CARLETON: No, Miss Smarty. *(Picking up the pitcher)* I wanna propose a toast first.

JOSEPH: Aw, man, I'll never eat.

CARLETON: *(Pouring into cups)* Just one toast, Little Joe, okay?

CARLENE: *(To* CARLETON*)* You didn't put no liquor in this Kool-Aide, did you?

CARLETON: Naw, Mama, just ginger ale. I swear. Okay, now take up your cups.

(Everyone lifts their cups.)

CARLETON: To us. A family. No matter how you slice it.

(For a moment everyone is speechless.)

CARLENE: That's so nice, Carleton.

(They clink cups and drink as spotlight goes out on FRANKLIN, *who exits.)*

JOSEPH: *Now* can it eat?

CARLETON: Knock yourself out.

CARLENE: *(Heading out)* Ice cream.

JOSEPH: Hope you got chocolate, Grandma.

CARLENE: You know I do, sugar.

CARLETON: *(Teasing)* Yeah, anything for "the Sugar".

JOSEPH: *(Embarrassed)* Aw, man.

CARLETON: "Aw, man."

WANDA: *(Playfully)* Leave my son alone.

CARLETON: Hey, *my* nephew can take it.

JOSEPH: Will y'all quit fightin' over me.

(CARLETON *and* WANDA *turn to* JOSEPH *and begin playfully beating on him and laughing.*)

JOSEPH: Hey, hey, stop it, y'all, stop it. *(Calling)* Grandma!

(*Lights fade out as* CARLETON *and* WANDA *chase* JOSEPH *off laughing and kidding.*)

(*After a moment,* BATTLES *and* FRANKLIN *are heard S L in the dark.* FRANKLIN *is a little drunk.*)

FRANKLIN: Took me a whole damn hour to find your place, you know.

BATTLES: So where *were* you?

(*Lights come up S L on* BATTLES' *den as he and* FRANKLIN *enter.*)

FRANKLIN: 'Nother world, Battles, goddam 'nother world.

BATTLES: Yeah?

FRANKLIN: Lost as can be, man. Shoot, had to ask some fool on a corner. Hillcrest. You know Hillcrest?

BATTLES: Yeah, I know it. Rough neighborhood.

FRANKLIN: Damn straight.

BATTLES: What the hell were you doing there?

FRANKLIN: Finally? Drinkin'. Drinkin' in some damn bar.

BATTLES: Is that a fact?

FRANKLIN: Yeah. Orsey's Bar.

BATTLES: Orsey's?

FRANKLIN: The "D" was out.

BATTLES: Say what?

FRANKLIN: The neon.

BATTLES: Oh.

FRANKLIN: Not my kinda place really.

BATTLES: Yeah, well, you could've come here first and *then* gotten drunk.

FRANKLIN: *(Staggering a little)* I'm not drunk.

BATTLES: Oh, my mistake.

(BATTLES waits for FRANKLIN to say something, but FRANKLIN simply weaves in place.)

BATTLES: You gonna tell me about it or what?

FRANKLIN: Didn't work, Battles.

BATTLES: What didn't work?

FRANKLIN: Trying to see her.

BATTLES: Who?

FRANKLIN: Carlene.

BATTLES: Who's Carlene?

FRANKLIN: Wanda's mother.

BATTLES: And who the hell's Wanda?

FRANKLIN: Goes to City College. Part-time at night. One kid. Divorced. Sincere. Beautiful lady. Thirty-five years old. Thirty-five years old today.

BATTLES: Wait a minute, man. Slow down.

(FRANKLIN stops weaves.)

BATTLES: Don't tell me you've been stepping out on Diane.

FRANKLIN: *(Laughing)* Stepping out? Who the hell you think I am anyway? *You?*

BATTLES: *(Not amused)* Then I don't get it.

FRANKLIN: Neither did I at first. I'd just gone by to see her, gone by to…I don't know. And that's when I heard laughter, singing. But I just didn't get it. So I pressed my ear up close to the door to find out. Slinkin' around like a dirty ole man. Hell, I coulda been arrested or somethin'. Blown away. *(As if reading a headline)* "Man blown away tryin' to break into his own past."

BATTLES: You're not making sense.

FRANKLIN: Didn't go, of course. Didn't go in, I mean, 'cause everybody was singing and happy and I was...

(FRANKLIN laughs drunkenly.)

BATTLES: Man, will you quit this screeching and tell me what this is all about?

(FRANKLIN takes a moment.)

FRANKLIN: *(Soberly)* She's my daughter. Wanda's my daughter.

(Now BATTLES takes a moment.)

BATTLES: What?

FRANKLIN: She doesn't even know it. But I know.

BATTLES: You do, huh?

FRANKLIN: Damn straight. Besides, her mother's name's Carlene.

BATTLES: *(Sarcastically)* Oh, well, that explains everything.

FRANKLIN: I remember, you know.

BATTLES: Damn, Franklin.

FRANKLIN: I do remember some things.

BATTLES: Shit, man.

FRANKLIN: It ain't all a blank. I've got it. *(Placing a finger to his head)* Up here.

(Jazz music from the late 1940's comes up softly.)

FRANKLIN: Hear that?

BATTLES: What?

FRANKLIN: Music.

(BATTLES *listens but doesn't hear any music.*)

BATTLES: What music?

FRANKLIN: Yeah. Music all right. Jazz. Circa nineteen forty-eight. Her heart's blood, she said... Yeah. This dingy, funky little apartment up some ole back stairs. Woo-wee, what a musty, lived-in smell. But then this other smell, too. Sweet smell of a girl, a woman. Heart-pumping smell. Like bein' engulfed, charmed. Young snake stiff as a rod. Music playin' all up and down it like it knew it by heart. Wrapped around. Itchin', desperate to know. You know what I'm talkin' about, what I'm sayin'. You've been there, right? Tiny, bumpy ole sofa. Just little pinches of light in the room... "I don't know, Carly," I say, "I don't know." "Don't you want to?" she says. "Yeah, I want to, I want to real bad, but—" "Then it's okay, sugar, it's okay." Sugar, sugar, sugar. Sweet, sweet sugar. Honey overflowin', sticky, mixin' with... Yeah. Thirty-five years ago, man. Thirty-five years. Yeah, I remember.

(*Lights come up S R on young* CARLENE [CARLY], *who is waiting impatiently and nervously in a wooded area. She wears a simple dress and sweater. It is early spring of 1948, and she is seventeen years old. [Note:* CARLY *is played by the actress who plays* WANDA.*]*)

(*The lights fade out on* BATTLES *and* FRANKLIN. *The music fades out as well.*)

(*After a moment* CARLEY *hears something in the distance. Soon young* FRANKLIN [FRANKIE] *enters. He wears a light coat and a cap. [Note:* FRANKIE *is played by the actor who plays* BOBBY.*]*)

FRANKIE: Sorry, Carly. I just couldn't get over here any sooner.

CARLY: That's all right.

FRANKIE: You been waitin' long?

CARLY: *(Lying)* No.

(They just look at each other for a moment.)

FRANKIE: *(Impatiently)* Well, what—

CARLY: Ain't you gonna kiss me?

(FRANKIE kisses CARLY.)

CARLY: I been missin' you.

(FRANKIE simply sighs.)

CARLY: Ain't you been missin' me?

(FRANKIE says nothing.)

CARLY: You don't come 'round to Frieda's no more.

FRANKIE: My daddy don't like for me to be hangin' out in such places.

CARLY: I don't mean no "hangin' out. .I mean just come 'round from time to time.

FRANKIE: What's the dif... *(Sighing)* I don't want to.

(Slight pause)

CARLY: How you been?

FRANKIE: All right.

(Slight pause)

CARLY: How's—

FRANKIE: Look, it's kinda late, Carly. And it's a little cold out here, too. What do you want that's so all-fired important?

CARLY: I don't know why it is you gotta talk to me that way.

FRANKIE: What way?

CARLY: I just don't know why.

FRANKIE: I don't know what you talkin' about.

CARLY: I know. I know you don't.

FRANKIE: What's the matter? You in some kinda trouble with your mama?

CARLY: No.

FRANKIE: You didn't run away or anything, did you?

CARLY: Run away?

FRANKIE: Yeah. I mean, you're always talkin' about how mean your mama is to you. How you wish you could just get away from here. So I thought—

CARLY: You see a bag?

FRANKIE: *(Looking around briefly)* No, I—

CARLY: So how you figure I done run away from home without no bag?

FRANKIE: I was—

CARLY: How that sound to you?

FRANKIE: I was just—

CARLY: Crazy. That's how it sounds. Anyway, seems to me *you'd* be the one to be runnin' away from here.

FRANKIE: Me?

CARLY: *(Whiny)* "He don't understand me, Carly. My daddy just don't understand me sometimes."

FRANKIE: *(Embarrassed)* That's private, Carly. Private. You don't have to be throwin' it up in my face like that.

CARLY: You done thrown mine up in mines.

FRANKIE: I was just tryin' to find out why we standin' out in the woods like this in the middle of the night.

CARLY: It ain't the middle of the night.

FRANKIE: Now look—

CARLY: I'm pregnant.

(FRANKIE is stunned.)

FRANKIE: You're…you're what?

CARLY: Pregnant.

(FRANKIE *thinks for a moment.*)

FRANKIE: What…what's that got to do with me?

CARLY: What's that got to— Don't you be sayin' that to me, Frankie Thompson.

FRANKIE: It can't be me. Uh-uh. It just can't be.

CARLY: Why not?

FRANKIE: 'Cause it was my first time. My first and only time.

CARLY: *Any* time can be the time. Don't matter if it was your "first and only" or not.

FRANKIE: But I— *(He paces for a moment.)* How do you know you're pregnant?

CARLY: I just know, that's all.

FRANKIE: And who else knows?

CARLY: Nobody else.

FRANKIE: Durnit! …I wasn't even supposed to be there.

CARLY: Don't matter much now 'cause you was.

FRANKIE: You practically had to drag me up those stairs.

CARLY: That's a lie, Frankie Thompson, and you know it. We both knew my mama and sister wasn't gonna be home, even if we didn't say it out loud to each other.

FRANKIE: But my first time.

CARLY: There coulda been other times, you know. There coulda been. You the one done run out.

FRANKIE: I just didn't think we should be seen together anymore.

CARLY: After we done been so close, you mean.

(FRANKIE *says nothing.*)

CARLY: And why is that? You hate it so much?

FRANKIE: No, I—

CARLY: What'd you do? Throw up all over yourself once you got clear of the house?

FRANKIE: No, I loved it. You should know that. I loved it...so much.

CARLY: But not me.

FRANKIE: I ain't say that.

CARLY: I was just a raggedy ole practice doll for Reverend Thompson's son, right?

FRANKIE: No.

CARLY: Kinda like them white boys from the master's house ruttin' with my great grandmamma down on the plantation so's they could—

FRANKIE: No! (*He begins pacing again and "speaking to the heavens."*) No, no, no. God, no.

CARLY: (*More sympathetic now*) Frankie.

FRANKIE: No, please, God, please.

CARLY: I'm sorry, Frankie.

FRANKIE: Not to me.

CARLY: I didn't want—

FRANKIE: It's not fair.

CARLY: I didn't want this to happen.

FRANKIE: You're not playin' fair with me.

CARLY: I didn't want it to turn out this way.

FRANKIE: Oh, man!

CARLY: What we gonna do, Frankie? What we gonna do?

(After a moment FRANKIE *stops his pacing and refocuses on* CARLY.)

FRANKIE: Wait a minute… How come you so sure I'm the father?

CARLY: How come?

FRANKIE: Yeah. I mean like it wasn't *your* first time. That's for sure. So how come you so sure I'm the one?

CARLY: 'Cause I ain't no slut, you hear me?! I ain't no slut and I ain't dumb!

FRANKIE: Then you must have done it on purpose.

CARLY: What you talkin' about? We *both* done it.

FRANKIE: You know what I mean.

CARLY: We took a chance. We both took a chance.

FRANKIE: But I didn't know.

CARLY: You didn't care, you mean.

FRANKIE: I did care. I *did*.

CARLY: Then what you fixin' to do now?

*(*FRANKIE *hesitates for a moment.)*

FRANKIE: What *can* I do? I'm graduatin' in June, goin' to college in the fall.

CARLY: Humph.

FRANKIE: No, listen to me. I'm goin' to be studyin' for the ministry one day soon. Don't you understand?

*(*CARLY *turns away from* FRANKIE. *He pursues her.)*

FRANKIE: I've got to do it. I need to. It's important to me.

CARLY: *(Turning on him)* No, it ain't. It's important to your daddy. You all of a sudden *makin'* it important to you just so's you can talk yourself outta doin' what's right.

FRANKIE: That's not true. I swear.

CARLY: Ain't no need to be swearin' it. You's in enough trouble already.

FRANKIE: Carly, I can't...I can't be responsible for this. I just can't.

(CARLY *waits for a moment to see if* FRANKIE *will continue.*)

CARLY: And so?

FRANKIE: Carly, please, please, whatever you do, keep me out of it. Keep my name out of it.

(CARLY *says nothing.*)

FRANKIE: Please, I beg you. I'll do anything you want. Anything but—

(CARLY *still says nothing.*)

FRANKIE: Well, why can't you blame it on...on one of your boyfriends or something?

(CARLY *is truly hurt by* FRANKIE'*s question.*)

CARLY: I thought...I thought *you* was my boyfriend. On the sly maybe, but my boyfriend, nonetheless... Anyway, there ain't nobody else right now. Not really. Not that I felt so happy to be seein' just walkin' down the street. Not that I been so crazy to be touchin' all over with my hands. *(She hugs him tightly.)* Nobody else, Frankie. Nobody else like that. It's the truth. The God's-honest truth. It's you, Frankie. I love *you*. I do. I swear I do.

(FRANKIE *slowly and very deliberately takes* CARLY'*s arms from around him.*)

FRANKIE: Franklin. My name is Franklin. Franklin Thompson the Third. Nobody calls me Frankie anymore. Nobody but you.

(CARLY *backs a few steps away from* FRANKIE, *staring at him coldly.*)

CARLY: (*Matching his deliberateness*) You're a coward, Franklin Thompson the Third. A lyin', snivelin', selfish, little boy coward. And you's gonna make the worst preacher there ever was. (*She turns to go.*)

FRANKIE: Wait. What you gonna do?

CARLY: (*Turning back to him*) Oh, don't you worry none. I'll take care of it. *Me.* My *ownself.* And I'll never mention your precious little name neither. And not 'cause I wanna help you out none. It's 'cause I don't want no child of mine to know that a boy like you ever existed, much less that he was his daddy. (*She runs off.*)

FRANKIE: (*Calling*) Carlene… (*Almost to himself*) I'm sorry.

(FRANKIE *stands alone, stunned, in the wooded area. The lights narrow to a spotlight on him as another spotlight comes up on* FRANKLIN *in* BATTLES' *den.*)

FRANKLIN: Dammit!

(*Spotlight goes out quickly on* FRANKIE, *who exits, just as the lights come back up fully on* BATTLES' *den.*)

FRANKLIN: I should have known it was her birthday! I should have known it!

BATTLES: Well, you didn't, all right? So stop beating yourself up, for Christ's sake. Besides, what if you *had* known? What would you have done? Gone charging in there with a big Teddy bear or gold earrings or something saying, "hi, everybody, sorry I'm so late, by the way I'm your daddy, Wanda"?

FRANKLIN: (*Flopping down in a chair*) No…no.

(*Slight pause*)

BATTLES: Franklin. Franklin, Franklin, Franklin. Good buddy.

(FRANKLIN *softly begins to sing a Baptist hymn.*)

FRANKLIN: We are soldiers in the Army.
We've got to fight although we have to cry.
We've got to hold up the bloodstained banner.
We've got to hold it up until we...
(*He keeps the word "die" to himself.*) The thing is...the
thing is, see. You've got this powerful preacher of a
father who, among other things, writes sermons that'll
sear your eyes if you get too close to the pages they're
written on. And he's telling you how he wants you to
be a preacher just like him 'cause, after all, *his* daddy
was a preacher, and you *are* the only son in the family,
sandwiched, as it were, between two older sisters and
a precious younger sister who's the apple of daddy
preacher's eye. And you find yourself almost blindly
saying yes, yes, I want to, I need to, I must. It's a part
of me, a part of us. And yet all the while some tiny
little demon inside you is saying, no, uh-uh, 'cause
you're nervous half the time, hesitant, scared. And you
begin dreaming about running away, escaping to all
the places you read about in novels and stories 'cause
for you the world of books, the world of provocative,
silently breathing words, is perhaps the most precious
of all... And then this girl. This beautiful, fun-loving
girl you meet on the street one day. Just by chance.
Carlene Humphrey. And for the first time in your life
you feel sooo...good. (*Speaking as his father*) You'd
better cut that girl loose, boy. Just cut her loose. You're
barkin' up the wrong tree. Travelin' in the wrong
circles. You've got yourself a name, a reputation.
You've got yourself someplace to go. Someplace
special! You gotta stay *on* track, not *across* the tracks!
(*Pause. Back as himself*) I'm gonna keep seeing her,
Battles.

BATTLES: Why?

FRANKLIN: Because there's no other way.

BATTLES: Yes, there is. You could let it go. Just let the whole goddam thing go.

FRANKLIN: No.

BATTLES: I'm telling you, man. You've got to stop this digging into your past like this. You've got to go forward.

FRANKLIN: I *am*.

BATTLES: With Diane, Bobby. But leave this other stuff alone. Leave it alone before it blows up in your goddam face.

FRANKLIN: I can't… The right turn, man. I'm making the right turn.

BATTLES: Are you sure about that?

FRANKLIN: Yes!

BATTLES: Then you've got to tell her, good buddy. You shouldn't keep fooling her. You've got to tell Wanda that you're her father.

(The idea of confessing that to WANDA *is still quite frightening to* FRANKLIN.*)*

(The lights fade out.)

END OF ACT ONE

ACT TWO

(*The music rises. Then the lights come up on* FRANKLIN *in his study. He stares D S. Suddenly, the music segues into the booming voice of* FRANKLIN'*s preacher father.*)

FRANKLIN THOMPSON JR: (*V O*) I don't know about you, boy. Where's your head? Where're you in that stubborn head of yours? Where do your eyes go sometimes when I look at you?

(FRANKLIN *takes a moment to think about what he's just heard in his head. Then he takes out a piece of paper, picks up the telephone, and dials the number that's on the paper. The telephone rings a couple of times U L in* CARLENE'*s living room as lights come up there.*)

CARLENE: (*Entering*) Hold your water. I'm not Wilma Rudolph, you know. (*Picking up the receiver*) Hello.

(FRANKLIN *says nothing.*)

CARLENE: Hello?

FRANKLIN: Carlene?

CARLENE: Yes, this is Carlene.

(FRANKLIN *says nothing.*)

CARLENE: Who is this?

FRANKLIN: (*Hesitantly*) Someone who...

CARLENE: Who? (*She waits, then slams down the phone.*) Shoot.

(FRANKLIN *hangs up.*)

(*The lights fade out on* CARLENE's *living room and* FRANKLIN's *study as they come up on* WANDA, *sitting on the sofa in her living room. She's studying.* JOSEPH *staggers in, high on reefer.*)

JOSEPH: Yo, Mama, what up?

(WANDA *says nothing.*)

JOSEPH: Hey, now I know what you thinkin'. But you wrong. I *did* my homework. Honest to God. Wanna see? (*He opens drawer of end table.*) I stuck it up in here somewhere, I think. Science report. Experiment or somethin'. Leaves, trees. All I had tonight. No math or English or nothin'. I don't know why. Them teachers, they... Now where the hell is it? I thought sure... (*He stops his search.*) Ohhh, ho-ho, I know. *You* took it, right? Wanted to check it out. See if I did good. 'Cause I'm just in high school and you takin' them college courses. So you can help me out. Can—

WANDA: Go to bed, Joseph.

JOSEPH: Well, I mean—

WANDA: Go to bed before I say something that'll put me further away from you than your daddy has ever been.

(JOSEPH *exits into his room. Lights fade out on Wanda's living room as lights come up U R on* CARLENE's *living room.* CARLETON *is giving his mother some money.*)

CARLETON: Take it.

CARLENE: What is it?

CARLETON: What do it look like?

(CARLENE *takes the money and counts it.*)

CARLENE: A hundred dollars?

CARLETON: Yep. Payback time.

CARLENE: But—

CARLETON: Yeah, I know, I know. I owe you a couple hundred more. But I be gettin' to it one day soon. Don't you worry.

CARLENE: Where'd you get this money, boy?

CARLETON: Where'd I— What you think I do? Rob me a bank or somethin'? I *do* work, you know.

CARLENE: Uh-huh.

CARLETON: All right, all right, I got lucky.

CARLENE: At what?

CARLETON: Never mind at what. Five bills there. Five sold Andy Jacksons. 'Course, I had me a few other debts, so I— And I don't have enough for California yet but— *(He gives her a big kiss on the cheek.)* There. Will that hold you for a while?

CARLENE: Go away from here, boy.

CARLETON: You just gotta trust me sometimes, Mama, that's all.

CARLENE: *(Sarcastically)* Trust you, all right.

CARLETON: See there? *Attitude.* Now if I be coppin' an attitude like that you be all up in my face and shit.

CARLENE: Carleton.

CARLETON: Stuff. All up in my face and stuff. *(He smiles.)* Now say you love me.

CARLENE: How you sound.

CARLETON: I just knew you did. *(Kissing her again on the cheek)* Gotta go. *(Heading out)* Don't spend that all in one place. *(Turning back)* You know somethin', Mama. Eddie's—

CARLENE: Eddie's what?

CARLETON: Eddie's still in my heart. But I got me places to go, things to do, you know?

(CARLETON *exits. Lights fade out on* CARLENE's *living room as lights come up D C on a corridor of a floor at City College.* FRANKLIN *and* WANDA *are walking and laughing together.* FRANKLIN *carries his briefcase,* WANDA *her books. Meanwhile at another end of the corridor* BATTLES *enters and stops to watch* FRANKLIN *and* WANDA, *unbeknownst to them.*)

FRANKLIN: *(Quite relaxed)* So I finally said to him: "Mister Grumski, the writing topic 'pet peeves' has nothing to do with why your cat freaks out when your mother tries to pick him up."

(WANDA *laughs, then causally touches* FRANKLIN's *arm.*)

WANDA: Why am I laughing? That sounds like a mistake I'd make.

FRANKLIN: No, you wouldn't. You're much too intelligent for that.

(WANDA *keeps her hand on* FRANKLIN's *arm for a moment. Then, slightly embarrassed, she takes it away. She smiles at him. He smiles back.*)

WANDA: Thank you.

FRANKLIN: You're quite welcome… Til next time then?

WANDA: Yes, til next time.

(WANDA *heads down the corridor, past* BATTLES, *and exits.* FRANKLIN *notices* BATTLES *for the first time.* BATTLES *comes up to him.*)

BATTLES: What the hell are you doing?

(FRANKLIN *thinks to say something but finally can't.* BATTLES *moves away from him, leaving him standing alone in the corridor with his thoughts, and heads D S into his den as lights come up on* DIANE *there.*)

BATTLES: So what do you want me to tell you, Diane?

DIANE: That he's not fooling around.

(FRANKLIN *exits down the corridor and the lights fade out there.*)

BATTLES: All right. He's not fooling around.

(DIANE *just looks at* BATTLES.)

BATTLES: You don't believe me.

DIANE: No.

BATTLES: Would I lie to you?

DIANE: You lied to Vickie.

BATTLES: Would I lie to *you*? About Franklin?

DIANE: You're best buddies.

BATTLES: Then why ask me in the first place?

DIANE: You're best buddies. *(Slight pause)* He's obsessed, Battles.

BATTLES: He's always obsessed.

DIANE: With more than just his work.

(BATTLES *says nothing.*)

DIANE: Work. I don't know. Maybe I've been too obsessed myself lately… What *is* this important work that we do anyway? Years of schooling, study, career advancement, networking, manipulating, and then nothing but work. When I finished law school, I told myself: at last, my own career. And then: me and Franklin. Two focused, educated, black professionals walking that narrow, precarious, golden path together. Money, convenience, status, some semblance of power.

BATTLES: Love?

DIANE: That's supposed to be a given.

BATTLES: Tell that to Vickie the next time you see her.

(Pause)

DIANE: I feel alone. No, lonely. *(Slight pause)* Who is it?

(BATTLES *says nothing.*)

DIANE: *Tell* me.

BATTLES: Not for me to say.

DIANE: Then you *do* know.

BATTLES: Not for me to say.

DIANE: You're a bastard.

BATTLES: I know. A thousand times over. But he's not fooling around.

(Slight pause)

DIANE: I'm scared.

BATTLES: It's gonna be all right.

DIANE: No, I don't think so.

(Lights fade out on BATTLES' *den and come up on* CARLETON *and* WANDA *in* WANDA's *apartment.*)

CARLETON: I *can't* ask Mama right now.

WANDA: Why not? *(Sarcastically)* You's her precious little baby.

CARLETON: *(Ignoring her remark)* I just paid her back for something.

WANDA: Looks to me like you done jumped the gun then.

CARLETON: Come on, Wanda. Just let me hold a hundred or so. I'll even take a check if you ain't got the cash on you.

WANDA: Oh, you will, will you?

CARLETON: Yeah.

WANDA: Why is everything always "money" with you?

CARLETON: Everything's not always—

WANDA: You're supposed to be "leading the family". Or so you say. Not being dragged by the nose by a "partner" you can't stop making—

CARLETON: I ain't bein' dragged by the nose by nobody. And everything's *not* always money with me. But how am I supposed to set myself up on the West Coast without money?

WANDA: Don't go.

CARLETON: Say what?

WANDA: It'd sure be a hell of a lot cheaper.

CARLETON: You trippin'.

WANDA: No, I'm just keepin' it real.

CARLETON: Okay, so why don't you quit college then?

WANDA: *(Incredulously)* What?

CARLETON: You heard me. Quit college. That'd be cheaper, too.

WANDA: Because I don't like standing still.

CARLETON: Ditto for me.

WANDA: There's no comparison.

CARLETON: The hell there ain't. You got a goal, and so do I.

WANDA: But *I'm* making it on my own.

CARLETON: Oh, is that so?

WANDA: Yes.

CARLETON: And what about the "buddy-buddy" professor dude of yours?

WANDA: What do you know about him?

CARLETON: That he's been "helpin' you out" a whole hell of a lot. Say he's a married man, too.

WANDA: Did Joseph tell you that?

CARLETON: Little Joe ain't no fool.

(WANDA *says nothing.*)

CARLETON: Well, least he's a brother.

(WANDA *still says nothing.*)

CARLETON: Hey, come on, Sis. Ain't no big deal. I mean, it's cool with me.

WANDA: You don't know what you're talkin' about.

CARLETON: Okay, okay, I don't, I don't.

(WANDA *just looks at* CARLETON *for a moment and then goes to her purse and takes out her checkbook.*)

WANDA: (*As she writes*) I'm writing you a check.

(CARLETON *smiles.*)

WANDA: For seventy-five dollars.

CARLETON: Seventy-five—

WANDA: That's it. The last check. And you can have it only on one condition.

CARLETON: And what's that?

WANDA: That you remember that Joseph is *my* son, not yours. And he's coming with me. Down *my* path. *Mine.*

(WANDA *holds out the check to* CARLETON. *He hesitates. Then finally...*)

CARLETON: Okay, Sis. Whatever you say. (*He takes the check. Putting it in his pocket*) But tell me something. How you gonna make him come with you? What you gonna do? Put him on a leash?

(*Lights fade out on Wanda's apartment and come up on* BOBBY THOMPSON, *a 23-year-old African American man, standing uncertainly in the middle of the* THOMPSON *home. He is* DIANE *and* FRANKLIN's *son.*)

(After a moment FRANKLIN *comes in carrying a small bag. He has been to the bookstore. He stops, clearly surprised to see* BOBBY *for the first time in more than a year. Father and son just stare at each other for a moment.)*

BOBBY: Hi, Dad.

FRANKLIN: Bobby… Well…you're home.

BOBBY: Yeah. *(Reaching for levity)* My key even works still.

(It falls flat with FRANKLIN.*)*

(Pause)

FRANKLIN: So…when did you get in?

BOBBY: About an hour ago.

FRANKLIN: Does your mother know?

BOBBY: Not yet.

FRANKLIN: She'll be so happy to see you.

BOBBY: Good. I've missed her, both of you, so much.

FRANKLIN: She's, we've, missed you, too. *(Holding up his bag)* Listen, I need to…

BOBBY: Sure, okay.

*(*FRANKLIN *goes into his study as he speaks, taking the books he's bought out of the bag and getting things together for his drive to City College, rearranging things and stuffing them in his briefcase.* BOBBY *follows him but stops at the study "door".)*

FRANKLIN: I'm teaching at City College this year.

BOBBY: Mom told me that last time I talked to her.

FRANKLIN: Yeah… I didn't see that car of yours outside.

BOBBY: I sold it. I was low on cash.

FRANKLIN: Oh, I see.

BOBBY: I hitch-hiked most of the way.

FRANKLIN: Why? Your mother and I could have sent you some money.

BOBBY: I know. But I figured I owe you too much already. *(Slight pause. Searching for the right words)* Dad...I want to apologize again for what I did. Wrecking your study like that. I was just stupid, crazy.

FRANKLIN: That you were.

(Packed briefcase in hand, FRANKLIN comes out of his study, BOBBY still waiting just outside the door. They stand before each other, almost as though BOBBY were blocking FRANKLIN's exit. After another awkward moment, FRANKLIN sets down his briefcase and hugs BOBBY, somewhat tentatively. Then he steps back from his son and picks up his briefcase.)

FRANKLIN: Well...I've got to get on the road. Your mother should be home this evening. *(Heading out)* In fact, why don't you call her now? I'm sure she'd drop everything and—

BOBBY: Dad.

FRANKLIN: *(Turning back)* Yes?

BOBBY: I sold most of my stuff in California. The rest is sort of in storage with a friend. Already got a line on a new job in the area. Looks pretty good, too.

FRANKLIN: What sort of job?

BOBBY: Sales. Department store.

FRANKLIN: Oh.

BOBBY: It's decent work, Dad.

FRANKLIN: Yes...decent.

BOBBY: I also plan to look for a place to stay.

FRANKLIN: You're welcome to stay here for as long as you need to.

BOBBY: Thanks.

(FRANKLIN *exits.* BOBBY *turns to the study "door". He takes a tentative step toward it, then steps back and turns away.*)

(*The lights shift, indicating a short passage of time, and then* DIANE *enters from behind* BOBBY.)

DIANE: Bobby!

BOBBY: *(Turning)* Mom!

(BOBBY *and* DIANE *embrace, holding on to each other as if for dear life.*)

DIANE: It's so, so good to see you.

BOBBY: It's good to see you, too, Mom.

DIANE: I've missed you so much.

BOBBY: I've missed you, too.

DIANE: I couldn't believe it when you called.

BOBBY: Hope I didn't take you away from some important murder case or something.

DIANE: I could murder you for "sneaking" home like this. It's been weeks since we last heard from you. And your phone number kept on changing so I couldn't—

BOBBY: There was too much stuff I had to sort out on my own. I'm sorry.

DIANE: I forgive you. Sorta. *(She hugs him tightly again and gives him a big kiss on the cheek. Then she steps back.)* Robert Alvin Thompson. *(Shaking her head)* Um, um, um.

BOBBY: What's wrong?

DIANE: You're too skinny.

BOBBY: No, I'm not.

DIANE: You haven't been eating.

BOBBY: Yeah, I have. All the food groups. I even quit smoking.

DIANE: Good. *(Slight pause)* How are you? Really?

BOBBY: I'm fine, Mom. Really.

DIANE: *(Not completely convinced)* Bobby.

BOBBY: Well...close to fine anyway.

DIANE: Was it rough?

BOBBY: Sometimes, Mom, yeah. Really rough. It was like I suddenly didn't know what to do with my hands, or my head. But I had to do it out there. I needed that space.

DIANE: I'm really proud of you.

BOBBY: Thanks.

DIANE: What'd your father say to you?

(BOBBY thinks for a moment.)

BOBBY: I hardly remember.

DIANE: *(Disappointed)* Well, he'll come around. The important thing is you're home.

BOBBY: It's good to be home.

DIANE: A family. Maybe we can be a family again.

(DIANE is thinking of FRANKLIN's absences. Meanwhile, lights come up on FRANKLIN and WANDA in WANDA's living room.)

BOBBY: What's the matter, Mom?

FRANKLIN: By the way, I brought you something. *(He takes a book out of his briefcase.)*

DIANE: *(Covering)* It's nothing.

BOBBY: Is it Dad?

WANDA: A book?

FRANKLIN: Yes.

DIANE: No, I'm just glad you've come home.

WANDA: Thank you.

FRANKLIN: You're welcome.

DIANE: Let me fix you something to eat.

BOBBY: No, I'm okay, Mom.

DIANE: *(Taking* BOBBY *by the arm)* Come on, your dad claims I don't cook anymore. We'll show him.

WANDA: *(Reading front cover of book)* African American Literature: Roots, Themes, and Progressions

*(*BOBBY *and* DIANE *exit as lights fade on the* THOMPSON *home.)*

WANDA: By Franklin Thompson the Third. *(Looking at* FRANKLIN*) Your* book.

FRANKLIN: Yes. A whole book.

WANDA: I'm really honored. And it's so beautiful.

FRANKLIN: Well, it's sort of old now, but I thought it just might be of some interest to you at some time or another.

WANDA: Of course. I can't wait to read it…I didn't know you were a "third".

FRANKLIN: Yes, I am. "The" third, rather. Hopefully not "a" third.

WANDA: I'm sorry. My durn English.

FRANKLIN: I was just teasing. You're fine. And your writing is really improving, really coming along. In just half a semester, too.

*(*WANDA *takes a moment, placing the book on the coffee table.)*

WANDA: Professor, I… Do you mind if I call you "Franklin"?

FRANKLIN: Of course not.

WANDA: Franklin, I really appreciate all the help you've been giving me. Going out of your way and all that. I think you're a really special person. Someone who's given me confidence in myself. Someone kind and patient and...and...

(WANDA *kisses* FRANKLIN. *Shocked and frightened,* FRANKLIN *pulls away quickly.*)

FRANKLIN: Wanda, no.

WANDA: I'm sorry.

FRANKLIN: No, I— *(He gets up.)*

WANDA: What have I done?

FRANKLIN: It's okay.

(WANDA *gets up.*)

WANDA: I got carried away. I'm really sorry.

FRANKLIN: No, it's not you. That is—

WANDA: You're married.

FRANKLIN: Yes. Also, I'm... That is...

WANDA: I'm so, so sorry. I was out of line.

FRANKLIN: Wanda, there's something...

WANDA: Yes?

FRANKLIN: I—

(*Suddenly,* JOSEPH *enters.* FRANKLIN *and* WANDA *turn away from each other guiltily. For his part,* JOSEPH *isn't at all happy to see* FRANKLIN *there.*)

WANDA: Well, it's about time you got home.

(JOSEPH *stares suspiciously.*)

WANDA: I assume you've done your school work.

JOSEPH: *(Not caring that he's lying)* Yeah.

FRANKLIN: How *is* school these days?

(JOSEPH *starts to exit into his room.*)

WANDA: Professor Thompson asked you a question.

JOSEPH: Great. Just great. *(He exits.)*

WANDA: I apologize for his rudeness.

FRANKLIN: I understand.

WANDA: He's just not used to seeing a man around here who's not his Uncle C.

FRANKLIN: Yes, well, I'd better get going.

WANDA: Listen, about that—

FRANKLIN: It's okay.

WANDA: I'll understand if you don't want to tutor me anymore.

FRANKLIN: Oh, no, no, I do. Although perhaps we should meet in my office from now on.

WANDA: Yes.

FRANKLIN: That would be better.

WANDA: Yes.

FRANKLIN: All right. Goodbye.

WANDA: Bye.

(FRANKLIN *exits as* WANDA *tries to sort through her feelings. She looks down at* FRANKLIN'*s book, then picks it up and begins looking through it. She finds an inscription in the front. She reads it.)*

WANDA: To Wanda. A wonderful, smart, certain to be college graduate. All the best in life. Franklin.

(JOSEPH *enters.*)

JOSEPH: What do you see in that guy anyway?

WANDA: I beg your pardon.

JOSEPH: He's old enough to be your father.

WANDA: Now that's enough.

JOSEPH: Well, he *is*.

WANDA: I said that's enough.

JOSEPH: Hangin' with an ole dude.

WANDA: We're not "hangin'".

JOSEPH: He's all the time over here.

WANDA: No, he's not. And what if he was? What I do with my life is my business, not yours.

JOSEPH: Well, we both gotta live here.

WANDA: I'm not hardly in your way as far as I can see. Especially since you're rarely here anyway.

JOSEPH: Well, it looks stupid.

WANDA: What does?

JOSEPH: You and him together.

(WANDA *is livid, but she at first controls herself by giving* JOSEPH *a long hard look.*)

WANDA: I am a grown woman, Joseph. Not just your mother. And I've got a life of my own to live. Now you're old enough to be understanding that. I've got things I want, things I need to do. To do for myself. I *want* to learn, to be in school. Even if you don't. And that "ole dude", as you call him, has been a big help to me, a real support. Now we're not gallivanting all around the place naked when he comes over here.

(JOSEPH *turns away embarrassed.*)

WANDA: Ain't no use in you being all embarrassed all of a sudden 'cause it's clear to me you done already thought it. Now I've done a hell of a lot for you. I've tried really hard. And if you don't like it, don't appreciate it, then you can just— *(Blurting out in frustration)* Dammit, Joseph! What the hell else do you want from me?!

(JOSEPH *is stunned. He takes a moment.*)

JOSEPH: Nothing, Mama. Not a goddam thing. (*He exits the apartment.*)

WANDA: Joseph. Joseph, come back—

(*Lights fade out on* WANDA's *apartment and come up on the* THOMPSON *home.* BOBBY *heads for* FRANKLIN's *study. He wants to speak to his father. When he gets to the "door", he stops and listens.*)

BOBBY: (*Calling*) Dad?…Dad, are you in there? (*He stands at the "door" for a moment. Then he looks around somewhat apprehensively. Finally, he enters.*)

(*It's the first time* BOBBY *has been in his father's study since he wrecked it more than a year ago. He looks around, walks around, takes everything in. After a while he slowly sits down at his father's desk. He runs his hands over the desk, first slowly, then faster and faster, around and around and around until he pulls his hands up and balls them into fists as though he's going to pound the desk. But he doesn't. Instead, he opens his hands and places them on the top of his head. He sits like that for a moment, breathing steadily, easily, as though bringing himself down from some manic state.*)

(FRANKLIN *enters the house still agitated about what happened at* WANDA's. *He heads straight for his study as though heading for his lair, his sacred place. When he enters the study he's shocked to see* BOBBY *there.*)

FRANKLIN: Bobby!

BOBBY: (*Jerking up from the chair*) Whoa!

FRANKLIN: What the hell are you doing in here?

BOBBY: You scared me.

FRANKLIN: Who said you could come in here?

BOBBY: I—

FRANKLIN: What do you want?

BOBBY: Hey, Dad, calm down, all right. I was just—

FRANKLIN: Have you been going through my things?

BOBBY: No!

FRANKLIN: Because the last time, you tore through here like some tripped-out tornado. Do you know how long it to me to recover some of those—

BOBBY: I didn't touch any of your stuff. Honest.

FRANKLIN: *("Straightening" things on desk)* Then what were you doing sitting at my desk?

BOBBY: I was just…I don't know.

FRANKLIN: *(Calming himself)* All right, all right.

BOBBY: What's going on, Dad? What's the matter?

FRANKLIN: Nothing.

BOBBY: Why are you so agitated?

FRANKLIN: I'm not agitated.

BOBBY: Then what—

FRANKLIN: Look, I don't have to tell you a damn thing, okay? You've been here, what, all of a couple of days and you think you—

BOBBY: I just wanna know, okay? I think I have a right to know.

FRANKLIN: And why is that?

BOBBY: *(Flippantly)* Oh, I don't know, Dad. 'Cause I'm your wayward only child maybe.

FRANKLIN: *(Sharply)* You're not— *(He just manages to stop himself from saying any more.)* Look, Bobby, I really need to be alone in here right now.

BOBBY: Of course. *(Indicating the study)* Here. Your lair.

FRANKLIN: My "lair"?

BOBBY: Heard you describe it that way to somebody somewhere once. *(In a whisper)* Gotta be getting back to my "lair." *(He takes a step toward the "door" to leave, then stops, making a conscious decision not to.)* You know what I used to do sometimes when I was younger, Dad? *(Not waiting for an reply)* Rub my hands all along your study walls. From the outside, I mean. It was like this game, this ritual. It was like I was trying to sense what was inside, what was going on inside. 'Cause when the door was closed and you were here alone, the space got a lot larger to me, the walls a whole lot thicker. They even seemed to shake, to vibrate in this crazy sorta way. To tingle like the whole study was this flying saucer hovering just above the Earth. Hovering and getting ready to take off. To leave at any moment. All its secrets lost to me forever...I think that more than anything else was why I wrecked this place. Your lair.

(FRANKLIN waits. Then...)

FRANKLIN: What do you want?

BOBBY: I want you to talk to me.

FRANKLIN: Are you high?

BOBBY: No.

FRANKLIN: Then what the hell's the matter with you?

(BOBBY studies FRANKLIN for an almost painfully long moment. Then...)

BOBBY: Who are you?

FRANKLIN: *(With a laugh)* Who am I?

BOBBY: Yes.

FRANKLIN: You're joking.

BOBBY: No, I'm not.

FRANKLIN: Okay, I'll play along. I'm a writer, a scholar, a college professor.

BOBBY: *(Looking around study)* So I see. *(He waits for more.)*

FRANKLIN: I'm a husband.

BOBBY: *(Pointing to the wedding band on his father's left hand)* So I see. *(Again, he waits for more.)*

FRANKLIN: And of course, I'm your father.

(BOBBY seems at a loss for anything to refer to for validation.)

BOBBY: And how do I know that?

FRANKLIN: *(Turning away in exasperation)* Game over, son. Goodnight.

BOBBY: *(Grabbing his father)* No, don't turn away from me.

FRANKLIN: What the—

BOBBY: Tell me!

FRANKLIN: Let go of me.

BOBBY: Tell me how I'm supposed to know!

FRANKLIN: Stop this foolishness!

(BOBBY and FRANKLIN are shouting.)

BOBBY: How am I supposed to know that you're my father?

FRANKLIN: *(Trying to wrench free)* I said stop it, dammit!

BOBBY: I want an answer from you!

FRANKLIN: *(Still trying to wrench free)* Stop it!

BOBBY: Not until you tell me.

(BOBBY knocks FRANKLIN hard to the floor. Then, immediately regretting it, he reaches down to help FRANKLIN up but his father waves him away.)

(Meanwhile, the shouting and ruckus have drawn DIANE *toward the study from the bedroom where she's been working. She enters just as* FRANKLIN *is picking himself up.)*

DIANE: What's going on in here? What happened?

*(*FRANKLIN *simply brushes himself off.* BOBBY *waits for his father to explain to* DIANE.*)*

DIANE: Franklin, what—

FRANKLIN: Nothing. I'm fine.

DIANE: Bobby?

BOBBY: Didn't you hear your writer, scholar, professor husband, Mom? He's fine.

*(*BOBBY *exits the study.* DIANE *stares at* FRANKLIN, *who says nothing. The lights fade out on* FRANKLIN'*s study and come up on* CARLETON *and* JOSEPH, *who enter and head for their park bench.)*

CARLETON: Why?

JOSEPH: 'Cause it's shit, Uncle C. Shit. I mean like when's my life supposed to begin anyway?

CARLETON: What do you mean "when"? What the hell you think you been doin' for sixteen years? Pushin' up daisies?

JOSEPH: Aw, man, shit, I thought you was down.

CARLETON: And I told you I couldn't raise the cash like I thought I could just now, all right?

JOSEPH: Which is why you should let me do it *my* way.

CARLETON: No.

JOSEPH: But Corey said it'd be smooth. Real easy.

CARLETON: No, goddammit. And that's that. You get all tangled up in that shit and you never be free.

JOSEPH: But it'd be just a delivery. Just one damn delivery.

CARLETON: Yeah, and soon you be all cracked up just like the rest of'em.

JOSEPH: And how you figure *that* if we gonna be layin' up on a beach in California, soakin' up the sun, scopin' out the chicks? I thought that's what you wanted.

CARLETON: Don't you be tryin' to mine the exact details of what I want. 'Cause that's much too deep down in my head, you hear?

JOSEPH: But two days ago you said you was goin' and that I could come with you.

CARLETON: If I could get the money together.

JOSEPH: And I'm sayin' *I* can get the damn money.

CARLETON: And I'm repeatin' that we not doin' it that way.

JOSEPH: Shit, later for you then.

(JOSEPH *starts to leave, but* CARLETON *blocks his way.)*

CARLETON: Where you goin'?

JOSEPH: Get outta my way, man.

CARLETON: Sit down.

JOSEPH: Why?

CARLETON: 'Cause I'm your uncle, that's why.

JOSEPH: So? You ain't got no money. You ain't got shit.

(CARLETON *smacks* JOSEPH.)

CARLETON: I said sit down, goddammit!

(*Stunned,* JOSEPH *sits down on the bench and just burns with anger.)*

CARLETON: Hey, look, man, like I'm sorry, but—

JOSEPH: Shit, I was crazy to come to your crib in the first place. Waitin' on you. Man, you don't know nothin'.

CARLETON: I don't, huh?

JOSEPH: Naw.

CARLETON: And how you figure that?

(JOSEPH *sucks on his teeth.*)

CARLETON: I ain't been nowhere, right?

(JOSEPH *says nothing.*)

CARLETON: Just 'cause I ain't hardly left this damn neighborhood don't mean that—

JOSEPH: I ain't say that. But it's not the same as when you was growin' up.

CARLETON: Shit, now I'm not *that* old, am I?

(JOSEPH *sucks on his teeth.*)

CARLETON: But you right, it's not. Not the same. Booby traps in the spaces *between* the damn booby traps now.

JOSEPH: Which is why I asked you to take me with you. And now you not even goin'.

CARLETON: If you so goddam itchin' to be goin', why don't you just go on by yourself?

(JOSEPH *says nothing.*)

CARLETON: I'll tell you why. 'Cause you scared, ain't you? ...*Ain't* you?

JOSEPH: And you *ain't* scared, I suppose.

(*Taken by surprise,* CARLETON *just lets* JOSEPH's *comment sink in.*)

JOSEPH: All I know is if I get blown up behind one of them damn booby traps it'll be on you.

CARLETON: Oh, it will, huh?

JOSEPH: Yeah.

(JOSEPH *sulks.* CARLETON *just looks at him for a moment.*)

CARLETON: You really wanna go, huh? Wanna make it outta here?

(JOSEPH *says nothing.*)

CARLETON: All right then. Le me lay this the hell on you. I promise I won't go to California without you. In fact, I'll even wait on you. How's that?

JOSEPH: Wait on me?

CARLETON: Yeah.

JOSEPH: Wait on me to do what?

CARLETON: Finish school.

JOSEPH: *(Getting up)* Aw, man—

CARLETON: No, listen. 'Cause this here's one hellified sacrifice I'm talkin' about. I mean three whole goddam years outta *my* life. And that's only providin' you don't be stayin' back again.

JOSEPH: Aw, man, you might not even *live* three more years.

CARLETON: You got that right. But then again *you* might not neither. So we both be takin' a chance. *(He smiles.)*

JOSEPH: Why you doin' this now? Sayin' this now?

CARLETON: *(Pointedly)* 'Cause you not me. You *can't* be me. You gotta stay clean, stay on top of things. I don't want you bein' the end of the line for the family. *(Slight pause)* So what do you say? Is it a deal? I mean a *real* deal?

JOSEPH: Man, I don't know. Seems like all my life is ever about is waitin'. Waitin' for this, waitin' for that. You see stuff you want slide on by and people say, no, no, not yet, wait, wait. And all the time other folks just be grabbin' and grabbin'. And laughin' at you while they be doin' it, too. "Chump." "Nigger." "Stupid motherfucker." That's all I am to a lotta—

CARLETON: No! Don't you say that. Don't you fuckin' say it. In fact, don't you even think it. *(Pause)* Tell you what. Why don't you go home tonight?

(JOSEPH sighs deeply.)

CARLETON: Come on. First step. I'll even go with you to back you up. Help you face my ole college-head of a sister. *Your* mother.

JOSEPH: Yeah? And what about *your* mother?

CARLETON: *(Half-jokingly)* Smart-assed little so-and-so, ain't you?

(JOSEPH smiles.)

CARLETON: Yeah, well, she'll probably be all up in it, too. So I guess I'll be facin' her sometime soon as well… So what do you say?

(JOSEPH thinks for a moment.)

JOSEPH: All right. I hate your damn cookin' anyway.

CARLETON: Me, too.

(CARLETON takes a pint of whiskey out of his pocket as the lights fade out on CARLETON and JOSEPH and come up on WANDA's living room just as CARLENE and WANDA are entering.)

WANDA: Not a word. Not one. Not even from his so-called friends.

CARLENE: And the police?

WANDA: Shoot, they looked at me like they was thinkin': well, he's sixteen, black, male, he must be into somethin' shady anyway so…Mama, I just—

CARLENE: *(Hugging WANDA)* It's gonna be all right.

WANDA: I just knew something like this would happen.

CARLENE: Try not to worry so much. He'll turn up, believe me.

WANDA: And what if he turns up dead?

CARLENE: Don't you be thinkin' like that.

WANDA: *(Pacing)* It's just been building up and building up. If it wasn't him not going to school, it was him smoking reefer or Professor Thompson coming over or—

CARLENE: Who?

WANDA: Professor Thompson. The teacher at City who's been tutoring me. I mentioned him to you.

CARLENE: Not his name.

WANDA: Well, it's Thompson. Franklin Thompson.

(While WANDA *presses on,* CARLENE *focuses on the name "Franklin Thompson".)*

WANDA: It's like my life and Joseph's life just keep pullin' at each other to no end. I wish I could—

CARLENE: This Franklin Thompson. You say he teaches at City College?

WANDA: Yes, Mama. A visiting professor.

CARLENE: What's that mean?

WANDA: He's only there for a year. Doesn't even live in town. Commutes from over in Monroe where he usually teaches.

CARLENE: *(Indicating* WANDA's *apartment)* And you say he's been coming over here?

WANDA: *(Somewhat guiltily)* Just a few times. Most times we meet in his office.

CARLENE: To do what?

WANDA: Go over my writing, Mama.

CARLENE: Why?

WANDA: Because I was getting "D"s, remember? And now I'm getting—

CARLENE: But why has *he* been helping you?

WANDA: *(Somewhat defensively)* Because he's a very nice man, that's way. Look. *(She gets FRANKLIN's book from a drawer of the end table.)* He even gave me an autographed copy of one of his books. *(Giving book to CARLENE)* African American Literature: Roots, Themes, and Progression.

CARLENE: *(Eyeing the cover suspiciously)* Franklin Thompson the Third.

WANDA: Yeah. A mouthful, ain't it?

CARLENE: What else has he been doin' for you?

WANDA: *(Embarrassed but covering)* Mama, the man's married.

CARLENE: Does he know who I am?

WANDA: Who *you* are? I don't know. Why would he want to… Well, come to think of it, he did ask me your name once, but—

CARLENE: And you told him?

WANDA: Yes. But that was the end of that.

CARLENE: Where'd you meet him?

WANDA: At City.

CARLENE: When?

WANDA: A couple of months ago.

CARLENE: What has he told you about hisself?

WANDA: Not much really. We've mostly talked about me. What's the big deal? What's any of this have to do with Joseph?

CARLENE: *(Momentarily confused)* Your father?

WANDA: No, my son. Remember?

(The door buzzer sounds, causing WANDA *to jump nervously.)*

WANDA: Oh, my God...I hope it's not the police.

CARLENE: You want me to get it?

WANDA: *(Bracing herself)* No.

(As the door buzzer sounds again, WANDA *exits to get the door. Meanwhile,* CARLENE *stares at* FRANKLIN's *book as memories race through her mind.)*

(After a moment WANDA *comes in with* FRANKLIN.*)*

WANDA: This is such a surprise.

FRANKLIN: Sorry I didn't call.

WANDA: That's okay. But I'm in sort of a crisis right now. Joseph is missing, gone.

FRANKLIN: Oh, no.

WANDA: Yes. My mother and I have been frantic.

*(*CARLENE *and* FRANKLIN *are quite surprised to find themselves face to face for the first time in thirty-five years.)*

WANDA: Professor Thompson. Uh, Franklin. This is my mother, Carlene Wallace. Mama—

CARLENE: Franklin Thompson the Third.

FRANKLIN: Hi, Carlene.

CARLENE: Frankie.

FRANKLIN: Yes.

WANDA: You know each other?

CARLENE: You might could say that.

WANDA: Wow. How? *(Silence)* Mama?

*(*FRANKLIN *waits for* CARLENE *to say something, but he soon realizes that he must finally speak the truth.)*

FRANKLIN: I'm...I'm your father, Wanda.

(WANDA *is speechless for a moment.*)

WANDA: What?

FRANKLIN: I'm your father.

WANDA: Mama?

CARLENE: He's right. He *is* your father.

WANDA: Oh, my God!

FRANKLIN: Wanda, I—

WANDA: Why? How...how is this possible?

FRANKLIN: I...I denied your mother when she told me she was pregnant. Just erased her from my life.

WANDA: And you knew it was me? All along? All this time you were helping me you knew?!

FRANKLIN: Your eyes. And then your mother's name.

WANDA: You used me!

FRANKLIN: No, I was helping you. Caring for—

WANDA: Caring?!

FRANKLIN: Yes. You said so yourself. You said—

WANDA: Yes, I said it. It was... You've been... But my *father*. To mess over me like this. Play with my feelings. *(Recalling the kiss)* And then when I— Oh, my God.

FRANKLIN: Wanda, I'm sorry. I am so, so sorry. I meant to tell you. Over and over again. I just didn't know how. But tonight I was—

CARLENE: Oh, yes, you did. *(She picks up* FRANKLIN's *book.)* With this. You thought to just ease on back in with this, didn't you?

FRANKLIN: No, you don't understand.

CARLENE: Just pick up right where you left off. So easy for you, so smooth.

FRANKLIN: No, that's not it.

CARLENE: And you not even a preacher.

FRANKLIN: Please, let me explain.

CARLENE: *(Slamming the book down)* No support, no real thought of me. Exceptin' maybe what I might could do for *you*. Just sneak on back in and claim *my* child without so much as a "pardon me". ...What the hell are you doin' in this place now? Why are you crowdin' me now?

FRANKLIN: I don't mean to—

CARLENE: My daughter all worried and upset. My grandson, my only grandchild, out on the streets missin' somewhere. And now here you come tryin' to—

FRANKLIN: *(Impulsively)* He's my grandson, too. My only grandchild, too.

*(*CARLENE *moves to strike* FRANKLIN. *But then she stops herself and simply seethes with anger.)*

FRANKLIN: I don't mean to crowd you, Carlene. I just want to try and help you for once in my life. Please. Please, let me help you if I can. *(With a look toward* WANDA*)* You and Wanda.

*(*CARLENE *says nothing.)*

FRANKLIN: Do you want me to go?

CARLENE: I ain't got no say in it here. This here's Wanda's place.

FRANKLIN: Wanda?

*(*WANDA *just stares at* FRANKLIN. *Then she moves to respond, but before she can,* CARLETON *is heard speaking loudly. It is clear that he has been drinking.)*

CARLETON: *(Offstage)* Naw, naw, now I told you I'd help you deal with it, didn't I? So just follow your Uncle C.

(CARLETON enters with JOSEPH almost in tow.)

CARLETON: Hey now, everybody.

CARLENE: Carleton.

CARLETON: That's my name. Don't wear it out.

WANDA: Joseph!

JOSEPH: Hi, Mama.

WANDA: Where in the world have you been, boy?

CARLETON: Safe and sound, Sis. Safe and sound.

WANDA: I thought I told you to leave Joseph—

CARLETON: The family can live on now 'cause Little Joe's come back safe and sound.

CARLENE: Where'd you find him?

CARLETON: On my damn doorstep.

JOSEPH: I've been stayin' with Uncle C.

CARLETON: *(Winking at JOSEPH)* Eatin' my food and everything.

WANDA: All this time.

JOSEPH: Mostly, yeah.

CARLENE: *(To CARLETON)* Why didn't you tell us?

CARLETON: 'Cause he asked me not to. 'Sides, we had a few things to work out.

CARLENE: What things?

CARLETON: Man-to-man type stuff, right Little Joe?

WANDA: *(To JOSEPH)* Boy, I ought to wring your neck.

CARLETON: Hey, now, cool it, Sis. He's back, ain't he?

WANDA: Yeah, and you're drunk.

CARLETON: Well…

JOSEPH: He wasn't all the time drunk, Mama.

CARLENE: *(To* CARLETON*)* Do you have any idea what your sister and me have been through?

JOSEPH: It wasn't Uncle C.'s fault, Grandma. It was me.

WANDA: And what exactly did this "me" think he was doin'?

CARLETON: Come on now, Sis, you too hard on the boy.

WANDA: Too *hard*?

CARLETON: That's one reason he left in the first place.

CARLENE: Now you just stay outta this, you hear?

CARLETON: Why the hell should I be stayin' outta it? He's *my* nephew. The onliest one I got around here. And I'm damn sure man enough to give the boy advice. In fact, we was—

JOSEPH: *(Finally focusing* FRANKLIN*)* What's he doin' here?

(Everyone now focuses on FRANKLIN.*)*

CARLETON: Who the hell *is* he anyway?

JOSEPH: That professor dude.

CARLETON: Ohhh. You mean the one that's been sniffin' up 'round your Mama.

CARLENE: All right now, Carleton.

JOSEPH: Yeah.

CARLETON: *(Going to* FRANKLIN*)* Well. Well, well, well, well, well. So what it is, Mister College Professor, Sir.

FRANKLIN: Hello, Carleton.

CARLETON: *(Mocking* FRANKLIN*)* Ohhh. Hello, Carleton. *(He laughs.)* And what might your name be, sir?

FRANKLIN: Franklin. Franklin Thompson the Third.

CARLETON: *(With a laugh)* Ohhh! My man's a third. And so where the rest of you go? *(To* JOSEPH*)* If it was ever there in the first place.

*(*CARLETON *cackles.* JOSEPH *can't help but laugh some himself.)*

FRANKLIN: *(Pointedly)* I'm Wanda's father.

*(*CARLETON *and* JOSEPH *abruptly stop laughing.)*

CARLETON: Huh?

JOSEPH: You're what?

FRANKLIN: Wanda's father.

JOSEPH: *(Caught in his imaginings)* Naw, naw, that can't be!

CARLETON: *(To* WANDA*)* Your *father?*

WANDA: Yes.

CARLETON: What the hell you talkin' about, girl? *(He goes to the photograph of Joseph, Senior in his Army uniform.)* That there's your daddy right there.

CARLENE: No, it isn't.

CARLETON: Who the hell was he then?

CARLENE: My first husband. But not your sister's daddy. You see I lied to her.

WANDA: No, Mama.

CARLENE: *(Turning to* WANDA*)* Yes. For thirty-five years. I kept him from you.

FRANKLIN: *(Stepping toward* CARLENE*)* I kept myself from her.

*(*CARLETON *steps abruptly between* CARLENE *and* FRANKLIN.)*

CARLETON: Don't you fuckin' touch my mother, Pops.

CARLENE: All right now, Carleton!

FRANKLIN: Take it easy.

CARLETON: This about as easy as I'm gonna get with you.

FRANKLIN: I think you should just cool down a little.

CARLETON: Cool down? Who the fuck you think you are anyway?

WANDA: Carleton!

CARLENE: Did you hear what I said?

JOSEPH: Come on now, Uncle C.

CARLETON: Some damn wanderin' knight ridin' in on his white horse to "save" my family?

FRANKLIN: Of course not.

CARLETON: Wanna be a fuckin' peacetime hero? Is that what you wanna be?

WANDA: Let it go, Carleton.

FRANKLIN: That's ridiculous.

CARLETON: You callin' me ridiculous?

FRANKLIN: No.

JOSEPH: It's okay, Uncle C.

CARLETON: You callin' me out my name?

FRANKLIN: No, I'm not here for that.

CARLETON: Then what the fuck you here for?

CARLENE: That's enough, Carleton.

FRANKLIN: To be who I am. Your sister's father. That's my connection to this family.

CARLETON: Connection?!

FRANKLIN: Yes. *(Going to* CARLETON*)* Now listen, son—

CARLETON: *(Jerking away)* I ain't your son, dammit! *(He begins pacing in a crazy, zigzag manner, his eyes ever on*

FRANKLIN.) My daddy's dead. Do you hear me? *Dead.*
Right along with the rest of'em. They all done just went
away and left me behind. And that's where folks all the
time be thinkin' I am, too. *Behind.* But I know different
now, 'cause I takes care of business, right, Little Joe?
I know where the family is, what it needs, right? I'm
"Pop" enough for everybody.

(CARLETON *staggers dizzily and falls to the floor.*)

CARLENE: Now just look at you.

WANDA: Carleton, please.

JOSEPH: Are you all right, Uncle C?

(*Seething with anger and a sense of humiliation,* CARLETON
simply stares up at everyone until his eyes lock on
FRANKLIN.)

CARLETON: (*Slowly rising from the floor*) Connection?
You can't make no damn connection here, you son of
a bitch. And you know why? 'Cause you ain't got the
key. *I'm* the one with the goddam key. The torch.

(CARLETON *takes his brother's knife out of his pocket and
opens it.*)

CARLENE: Put that durn thing away, boy.

CARLETON: I ain't no boy, Mama. (*Stepping towards*
FRANKLIN) You see, I got Eddie's name chiseled right
across my forehead.

WANDA: Chiseled?

CARLENE: What you talkin' about?

CARLETON: (*Ever focused on* FRANKLIN) What the hell
you got?

JOSEPH: (*Touching* CARLETON's *arm*) Come on now,
Uncle C. Ain't no need to be—

(*Impulsively,* CARLETON *swipes at* JOSEPH *with the knife,
but* JOSEPH *jumps back in time.*)

CARLETON: No!

WANDA: Oh, my God.

CARLENE: Are you hurt?

JOSEPH: No, I'm okay.

FRANKLIN: *(Moving quickly to* CARLETON*)* Are you out of your mind?! Give me that knife!

CARLETON: Here… *(Shoving the knife into* FRANKLIN*'s gut)* Take it!

(Everyone gasps. CARLETON *quickly pulls the knife out of* FRANKLIN *and turns away from him, closing and pocketing the knife.* FRANKLIN *grabs his stomach, placing his hands over the wound.* CARLENE *and* WANDA *go to* FRANKLIN. JOSEPH *doesn't know what to do.)*

WANDA: Franklin.

CARLENE: Frankie.

CARLETON: *(Somewhat dazed)* I gave it to him.

FRANKLIN: *(Waving them off)* I'm all right, I'm okay.

CARLETON: I gave it to him.

FRANKLIN: It's just a scratch. *(Showing his hands)* See? *(His hands are covered with blood.)*

CARLENE: Lord have mercy!

WANDA: You're hurt!

FRANKLIN: What?

*(*FRANKLIN *looks down at his hands and then staggers and falls to the floor.* CARLENE *and* WANDA *move to help* FRANKLIN *as* JOSEPH *remains somewhat petrified and* CARLETON *moves further away.)*

(Note: The dialogue begins to overlap.)

FRANKLIN: *(Disoriented)* What? What's going on?

WANDA: You're hurt.

CARLENE: You've been stabbed.

CARLETON: *(Noticing the blood)* What'd I do?

JOSEPH: Damn, Uncle C.

FRANKLIN: *(Trying to stand)* I've gotta get up.

CARLENE: *(Cradling FRANKLIN)* No, stay down, stay here.

WANDA: I'll call an ambulance.

CARLETON: *(Getting panicky)* Oh, man, what'd I do?

FRANKLIN: I'm sorry, Carlie. I'm really sorry.

CARLENE: You're gonna be okay, Frankie.

CARLETON: *(Yelling at FRANKLIN)* Get up, man! Get up!

JOSEPH: *(Pulling at CARLETON)* Stop it, Uncle C.

CARLENE: Get away, Carleton.

WANDA: *(Into the phone)* Yes, I have an emergency! A man's been hurt.

CARLETON: *(Moving around the room)* Damn you!

(JOSEPH tries to calm him down.)

WANDA: *(Into the phone)* What? ...Stabbed!

FRANKLIN: It kinda hurts, Carlie. Something hurts.

CARLENE: Don't worry, Frankie. You're gonna be okay.

WANDA: Seven-thirty-four Bolton Avenue. Apartment three-fifteen.

CARLETON: Why you doin' this, man?

JOSEPH: Give me the knife, Uncle C.

FRANKLIN: Why'd he do that, Carlie?

CARLENE: It's okay, Frankie.

WANDA: Yes, yes! Just hurry up! *(She hangs up the phone.)*

CARLETON: Oh, man, Eddie.

JOSEPH: Where's the knife?

WANDA: *(To* CARLENE*)* They're on their way.

FRANKLIN: Why'd my Daddy do that?

WANDA: What's he saying?

CARLENE: I don't know.

CARLETON: I didn't want this, man.

JOSEPH: I know, Uncle C.

FRANKLIN: *(Again trying to stand up)* I've gotta stand up, Daddy.

CARLENE: *(Keeping him down)* No, just lie still.

WANDA: The ambulance will be here real soon.

CARLETON: Oh, damn.

FRANKLIN: *(Struggling)* No, I need to stand up! I need to!

*(*FRANKLIN *slumps back into* CARLENE*'s arms.)*

CARLENE: Frankie! Frankie!

WANDA: No!!!!

*(*WANDA*'s "no" reverberates as the lights fade out on Wanda's apartment.)*

(There is a cacophonous swirl of music to indicate a passage of time. Then the lights come up on FRANKLIN*'s study.* BOBBY *and* WANDA *are there. They are both themselves and, through the reality of the actors' other portrayals, also the shadows of* CARLY *and* FRANKIE*.)*

WANDA: *(Trying to take everything in)* I never knew anybody who owned so many books.

*(*WANDA *focuses on* FRANKLIN*'s desk, touching it, running her hands along its top. Then she touches the chair, thinking about sitting in it.)*

BOBBY: Go ahead.

(WANDA *sits down in* FRANKLIN's *chair, soaks in the feeling of being there.*)

BOBBY: Dad was so at home here. I never really understood it. But something tells me you might have.

(A long pause)

WANDA: I've been wondering if I'll ever forgive him. *(Slight pause.)* My brother.

(BOBBY *takes that in.*)

WANDA: Always so obsessed he was. Obsessed with getting out, going to the West Coast, finding himself there, finding some new, other...self...

(Slight pause)

BOBBY: Several months ago I found myself sitting on top of this sand dune out there. Pismo Beach. Watching the sun set into the Pacific. Usually like a really beautiful sight. But this time I suddenly feel myself being pulled down, pulled in. It's like the sand has become this quicksand and that beautiful, bright-orange sun is helping it pull me in. And so I right away scramble, stumble to my feet. And although I'm still looking out at the water, at the waves curling in, brushing the shore, I'm really seeing behind me. Seeing behind me and saying to myself: Home...go home.

(*As* BOBBY *stands by and* WANDA *sits at their father's desk looking out, music rises and the lights fade out.*)

END OF PLAY